Colossians and

A Digest of Reformed

Colossians and Philemon

A Digest of Reformed Comment

GEOFFREY B. WILSON

MINISTER OF BIRKBY BAPTIST CHURCH
HUDDERSFIELD

THE BANNER OF TRUTH TRUST

THE BANNER OF TRUTH TRUST
3 Murrayfield Road, Edinburgh EH12 6EL
P.O. Box 621, Carlisle, Pennsylvania 17013, U.S.A.

*

© Geoffrey Backhouse Wilson 1980
First published 1980
ISBN 0 85151 313 1

*

Set in 11 on 12 pt Bembo
Typeset, printed and bound in Great Britain by
Hazell Watson & Viney Ltd,
Aylesbury, Bucks

CONTENTS

PREFACE

The warm welcome given to *Ephesians* leads me to hope that this treatment of the companion Epistles to the *Colossians* and *Philemon* may also be found useful. I am grateful to the authors and publishers who have kindly allowed me to quote from their works, and to the Evangelical Library, New College Library, and Dr. Williams's Library for the loan of various books. As usual the commentary is based on the American Standard Version (1901), published by Thomas Nelson Inc.

Huddersfield
February 1980

GEOFFREY WILSON

INTRODUCTION TO COLOSSIANS

The ancient city of Colossae was situated about 100 miles east of Ephesus in the Roman province of Asia (now Turkey), but in Paul's day its former glory had been eclipsed by the increasing prosperity of near-by Laodicea and Hierapolis. Although the apostle had not visited these cities of the Lycus valley [1.4; 2.1], such was the effect of his ministry at Ephesus that churches were established in each of them [4.13; *Acts* 19.10]. It would appear from 1.7 and 4.12f that the gospel was brought to this district through the labours of Epaphras (not to be identified with the Epaphroditus of *Phil* 2.25, 4.18), who was presumably converted to Christ through Paul's preaching. Epaphras later visited Paul during his Roman captivity, and it was his disturbing account of the situation in Colossae which prompted the apostle to write this Epistle.

As Paul gives no formal statement of the errors he opposes, it is impossible to determine the precise nature of the 'Colossian heresy', but it was evidently a form of syncretism which combined Jewish practices with pagan speculation. The Jewish element in this false teaching called for Gentile observance of the ritual requirements of the law [2.11, 16, 17], while its pagan element encouraged the worship of angelic intermediaries [2.18], and enjoined an asceticism which in its severe treatment of the body went beyond the law's demands [2.20–23]. This curious mixture was produced by the pride that discards divine revelation in favour of human reasoning

[2.8], and its inevitable result was the denial of that universal supremacy which belongs to Christ by the double right of creation and redemption [1.14–20]. The appearance of this novel doctrine was hardly a surprising development in a province which was so notorious for the variety and extravagance of its religious beliefs that not even the orthodoxy of the synagogues could be preserved from the prevailing corruption. It therefore seems likely that the Colossian errorists were resident Jews whose acceptance of these pagan notions made them more ready to change the gospel than to be changed by it. It is also apparent that their claim to superior 'knowledge' has certain affinities with later Gnostic teaching, but it is going beyond the evidence to interpret this early deviation from the faith in terms of the developed Gnosticism of the second century as R. McL. Wilson and Edwin Yamauchi have clearly shown.

The relation between Colossians and Ephesians is closer than that which exists between any other of Paul's letters. 'They are *twins*, the offspring of one birth in the writer's mind' (G. G. Findlay). But though these Epistles are so intimately connected that many verses are not only parallel but almost identical in content and style, they show a striking difference in the tone and treatment of their common themes. In Colossians Paul presents his readers with a reasoned defence of the gospel to ward off the threat posed to the church by false teaching, whereas in Ephesians he calmly reflects upon the glorious destiny which belongs to the church in virtue of her union with Christ. The fact that Ephesians lacks a credible 'life-situation' suggests that it was intended as a circular letter, and it is probably to be identified with the letter 'from Laodicea' which is mentioned in 4.16. Thus Paul, as a good physician of souls, sent the right antidote to counteract the poison of error (Colossians), and the right tonic to build up the faith of all believers in Asia Minor (Ephesians).

The brevity of Colossians is no index of its importance, for by unfolding the cosmic implications of Christ's absolute pre-eminence it directs us to trust in the sole sufficiency of his saving work. Although this doctrine is already expressed in germinal form in 1 Corinthians 8.6, it is here stated with greater precision and fulness than is found elsewhere in Paul's writings. As therefore this Epistle forms one of the peaks in the New Testament revelation of Christ, all who desire to reach a correct understanding of his Person must resolve to scale its heights.

The message of Colossians is that believers are complete in Christ, and that faith in him necessarily rules out reliance upon any subsidiary powers, for nothing in the entire universe lies outside the scope of his sovereignty. The contemporary application of this teaching should not escape us in a day when men everywhere are still held in bondage by forces they cannot control. For whether these powers are human or superhuman, none of these things 'shall be able to separate us from the love of God, which is in Christ Jesus *our Lord*' [*Rom* 8.39].

CHAPTER ONE

The apostle Paul associates Timothy with him as he salutes the saints at Colossae and invokes the blessing of God upon them [vv 1, 2]. He begins with thanks to God for the good account Epaphras had given him of their growth in grace [vv 3–8]. He prays that they might have the knowledge to walk worthily, and the strength to endure joyfully [vv 9–11]. They are also to give thanks to the Father, who qualified them for the inheritance when he delivered them from the realm of darkness and translated them into the kingdom of his beloved Son, in whom they are redeemed and forgiven [vv 12–14]. In the exalted language of worship Paul next sets forth the pre-eminence of Christ: He is the image of the invisible God, the source and sustainer of creation, the head of the church, and the reconciler of all things to himself [vv 15–20]. And the Colossians, though once estranged from God by evil works, were now reconciled through Christ's death and would be presented without blemish to God, if they continued to believe the gospel of which Paul was a minister [vv 21–23]. The apostle rejoices in his sufferings for the sake of Christ's church, as he fulfils his commission in making known to the Gentiles the once hidden mystery of the indwelling Christ, and strives to present every man perfect in Christ [vv 24–29].

V1: **Paul, an apostle of Christ Jesus through the will of God, and Timothy our brother,**

In introducing himself as an apostle 'through the will of God', Paul shows that his right to address a community of Christians to whom he is personally unknown is founded upon the distinguishing grace which made him the apostle to the Gentiles [2.1; *Eph* 3. 1ff]. As such he is clothed with the power of the Sender, who entrusted him with the commission to make known to all men 'the mystery of Christ'. And at the outset of an Epistle which stresses the pre-eminence of Christ, the word order of the title, 'an apostle of *Christ* Jesus', is probably intended to fix the attention of its readers upon the unique glory of their exalted Lord. With himself Paul associates Timothy, his own son in the faith [1 *Tim* 1.2], and a trusted helper and fellow-worker in the gospel [1 *Thess* 3.2], but who is here simply designated as 'the brother'. This sets him apart from the apostle as the author of the letter, and also provides a valuable endorsement of its message by a Christian who is well known in the churches.

*V*2: **to the saints and faithful brethren in Christ** *that are* **at Colossae: Grace to you and peace from God our Father.**

Although the Epistle is sent to the Christian community in Colossae, the word 'church' is omitted from the address, perhaps because Paul in his later years preferred to stress the character and calling which made its members Christ's witnesses in the world [cf *Rom* 1.7; *Eph* 1.1; *Phil* 1.1]. Thus their relation to God is indicated by the term 'saints', while their kinship with other believers is underscored by the word 'brethren'. The noun 'saints' recalls the electing grace which singled out Israel to be God's special possession [*Exod* 19.6; *Lev* 11.44], and its application to Christians identifies them as the people of the new covenant [1 *Pet* 2.9]. Sainthood is at once a gift and a vocation. What is first a *status* conferred, then becomes a *calling* to be followed [1 *Cor* 1.2]. But this response of faith is only made possible by the determinative act which preceded it. 'Saints are not an eminent sort of Christians, but all Christians are saints, and he who is not a saint is not a Christian' (Alexander Maclaren). In describing the brethren as 'faithful', it is not likely that Paul is hinting at the defection of some in Colossae as J. B. Lightfoot suggests [cf *Eph* 1.1], but the adjective more probably refers to the fidelity that is brought forth by the faith which embraces God's objective grace. As the vital phrase 'in Christ' here carries the deeper meaning of incorporation in Christ, it virtually defines the word Christian, and emphasizes the fact that salvation is found only in union with him.

The brief greeting conveys Paul's customary prayer for his readers. It is his wish that they may be blessed with grace and peace 'from God our Father', who is viewed as the ultimate source of this undeserved favour ('grace'), and of the spiritual prosperity ('peace') which results from it. And therein: 'He reproves the folly of this world, in which almost all wish for themselves and their friends, health, riches, and honours; but grace, peace, and other spiritual good things, they neither regard, nor think of. But Christ commands us to *seek first the kingdom of God, Matt* 6.33' (John Davenant).

*V*3 : We give thanks to God the Father of our Lord Jesus Christ, praying always for you,

We always thank God, the Father of our Lord Jesus Christ, when we pray for you, (RSV) That there was a church in Colossae was for Paul a cause of profound thanksgiving to God. As he knew that none could be saved without the regenerating grace of God [*Eph* 2.5], he never congratulates his readers on their faith, but always thanks God for it [cf *vv* 12, 13]. If we thus owe our salvation to God, then clearly all the praise must belong to him alone [1 *Cor* 1.29]. For when all the riches of God's grace are freely lavished upon us, we are under a permanent obligation to pay tribute to that grace in the coinage of our gratitude. The title 'the Father of our Lord Jesus Christ' serves to advertise the fact that God can only be savingly known through the self-giving love by which he has been pleased to reveal himself. For there would have been no good news to preach, if he had not sent his Son into the world to redeem us at measureless cost [*v* 14]. So whenever Paul prays for the Colossians, he always begins by thanking God for what he, the Father, has already done for them in Christ before presenting further supplications on their behalf [*v* 9]. We should seek to model our own prayers on this apostolic pattern, which teaches us that thanksgiving should always precede intercession.

*V*4: having heard of your faith in Christ Jesus, and of the love which ye have toward all the saints,

This gives the ground of the apostle's thanksgiving. Although he was not personally acquainted with his readers, he had received encouraging news of their faith and love from Epaphras, whose tireless labours had been the means of bringing the gospel to Colossae [*vv* 7, 8; 4.12]. As we have here two sure marks of a believer – faith in Christ and love to all the saints – those who lack them cannot rightly claim the name of Christian. The construction 'faith in (*en*) Christ Jesus' points not to the object of faith, but to the sphere in which faith lives and acts; for union with Christ is not only the source of life, but also the realm in which it is operative. Hence the expression focuses on the exalted Lord 'as the giver of new life to his people who live under his lordship' (R. P. Martin).

The fruit of this faith was seen in the love which the

Colossian believers had 'toward all the saints'. The reference is probably to the entire family of faith [v 6], for a real love for Christ must also embrace *all* who are his [1 John 4.7, 12]. The remarkable repetition of the word 'all' in this Epistle is evidently directed against the exclusiveness and caste-feeling which was fostered by the errorists' claim to superior knowledge [v 28]. This should teach us that there is no room in the church for any intellectual, spiritual, or social élite, which separates itself from fellow-believers whom Christ has accepted [3.11].

V.5: **because of the hope which is laid up for you in the heavens, whereof ye heard before in the word of the truth of the gospel,**

Both spring from the hope stored up for you in heaven (NEB) Hope completes the familiar triad of Christian graces which was probably part of the 'tradition' which Paul received from those who were 'in Christ' before him, but here hope is not co-ordinate with faith and love. It is rather represented as the *source* from which they spring. This hope is not a subjective attitude of expectation, but is the objective content of the gospel [v 23]. It is because the Colossians are assured that the *content* of the message they received is already stored up for them in heaven that they can remain firm in the faith and show their love to all the saints. Thus the future can be said to determine the present, for what is reserved in heaven for believers now exercises a decisive influence upon their daily conduct.

whereof ye heard before in the word of the truth of the gospel, There appears to be an implied contrast between the gospel they heard before from Epaphras and the false teaching which had since been presented to them. For they would forfeit their interest in the future, if the 'word of truth' by which this hope came to them was abandoned in favour of the false gospel of 'vain deceit' [2.8]. As the gospel is a word whose whole substance and content is truth, it is necessarily opposed to all the errors invented by men. 'The gospel is not speculation but fact. It is truth, because it is the record of a Person who is the Truth. The history of His life and death is the one source of all certainty and knowledge with regard to man's relations to God, and God's loving purposes to man. To leave it and Him of whom it speaks in order to listen to men who spin theories out of their own brains is to prefer will-o'-the-wisps to the sun' (Maclaren).

*V*6: **which is come unto you; even as it is also in all the world bearing fruit and increasing, as *it doth* in you also, since the day ye heard and knew the grace of God in truth;**

Paul gives thanks that the same message of salvation which had reached his readers in Colossae is also in all the world. His object in saying this is to excite their gratitude that the gospel had been sent to them, and to give them a salutary reminder of its universal scope [*v* 23]. The apostle's implication is that the universality of gospel truth must not be falsified and narrowed down to a sectarian heresy.

bearing fruit and increasing, As a tree both bears fruit and grows, so the gospel produces fruit in the conduct of believers [v 4] and also spreads by winning new converts. That the gospel has the reproductive power to spread throughout the whole world is due to the fact that God himself is at work in it [1 *Cor* 3.7].

as *it doth* in you also, since the day ye heard and knew the grace of God in truth; Paul thankfully acknowledges that the Colossians have also lived such fruitful lives from the day they learned what the gospel really is, and were glad to receive it as 'the grace of God' which brings salvation to the undeserving [*Tit* 2.11]. 'He praiseth, both their teachableness, in that this word had fructified in them, from the first day they heard it, and their constancy, for that it continued still fructifying to that time. The earth produceth not fruit, as soon as it hath received the seed: there must be time to mollify the grain; to make it thrust forth, and sprout; to raise it up, and garnish it with fruits. In this spiritual Husbandry, it is not so. The gospel, if rightly received into your heart, will fructify there, from that very moment' (Jean Daillé).

*V*7: even as ye learned of Epaphras our beloved fellow-servant, who is a faithful minister of Christ on our behalf,

In thus commending Epaphras to the Colossians Paul sets the seal of his approval on the teaching which he had delivered to them on the apostle's behalf. It was probably during Paul's stay at Ephesus that Epaphras acted as his representative in taking the gospel to Colossae [*Acts* 19.10]. Paul says two things about Epaphras which are worthy of note. First, he is 'our beloved fellow-servant' or 'fellow-slave'. Something of the warmth of Paul's character is brought out by this reference to the privilege of sharing together in the service of Christ. As the word 'slave' indicates, those who engage in this service have no will of their own, but are entirely under the direction of the Lord who redeemed them from the bondage of sin. Second, he is 'a faithful minister of Christ'. Since such fidelity is the very essence of true service, this commendation implicitly contrasts Epaphras with the false teachers 'in whom an opinion of their own wisdom predominated, when, nevertheless, they were unfaithful towards Christ' (Davenant).

*V*8: **who also declared unto us your love in the Spirit.**

Epaphras not only took the good news to Colossae, but also brought back to Paul a largely encouraging report of the progress of the new community. That the gospel had taken root in their lives was proved by the presence of the chief fruit of the Spirit [*Gal* 5.22]. It was through the Holy Spirit that the love of God had been shed abroad in their hearts [*Rom* 5.5], and it was this supernatural change which enabled them to love all the saints [*v* 4]. As love gives man his closest resemblance to God, 'and as it is the great object of the gospel to create and perfect it in the church, it may be safely taken as the index of spiritual advancement' (John Eadie). In view of the very full teaching on the Spirit which is found in Ephesians, it is rather remarkable that this is the only *explicit* reference to the Spirit in Colossians, but this is probably due to the apostle's desire to stress the absolute supremacy of Christ [*v* 18]. When Christ is so glorified we have the surest mark of the Spirit's presence, for the whole purpose of his coming is to exalt Christ [*John* 16.14].

*V*9: **For this cause we also, since the day we heard *it*, do not cease to pray and make request for you, that ye may be filled with the knowledge of his will in all spiritual wisdom and understanding,**

Paul's prayer for the Colossians is closely connected with the thanksgiving which preceded it [*vv* 3–8]. He is not only thanking God for their faith, but is *also* praying that they may continue to grow in grace [*vv* 9–12]. In thus revealing the content of his fervent intercession, he reinforces his exhortations, stimulates their aspirations, and teaches them how to pray. 'Since the day we heard' echoes 'the similar expression in verse 6. So the apostle's prayer was, as it were, an echo of their faith. An encouragement to them to proceed as they had begun' (T. K. Abbott).

that ye may be filled with the knowledge of his will As J. Armitage Robinson rightly points out, this is not knowledge in the abstract (*gnosis*), but 'knowledge' (*epignosis*) 'directed towards a particular object', which in this case is the knowledge of God's will as it relates to the conduct of our lives [*v* 10]. 'The apostle here made request for something intensely *practical*: not speculations about the divine nature, prying into the divine decrees, nor inquisitive explorations of unfulfilled prophecy, but the knowledge of God's will as it respects the ordering of our daily walk in this world' (Arthur W. Pink). Paul evidently intends to contrast the insubstantial flights of fancy canvassed by the false teachers with the true knowledge which leads to right behaviour.

in all spiritual wisdom and understanding, This knowledge of God's will is conveyed to believers in the form of all wisdom and understanding, and the emphatic position of 'spiritual' at the end of the verse shows that these are not natural virtues but gifts of the Spirit. 'Wisdom' is the practical ability to regulate conduct in the light of God's requirements, while 'understanding' is the capacity to apply this wisdom in every situation which demands a moral decision. For Paul these 'spiritual' gifts stand in direct contrast to the empty pretensions to 'wisdom' [2.23] which proceeded from 'the mind of the flesh' [2.18].

*V*10: **to walk worthily of the Lord unto all pleasing, bearing fruit in every good work, and increasing in the knowledge of God;**

This spiritual insight is to find concrete expression in the daily round and the common task. 'The end of all knowledge, the Apostle would say, is conduct' (Lightfoot). 'To walk' likens the Christian life to a journey towards heaven, which calls for unwearied advance along the path marked out for such pilgrims [*Is* 35.8]. The nature of this progress is specified in the summons to walk 'worthily of the Lord', as befits those who owe their whole salvation *to* him, and who can fulfil this high calling only in virtue of their union *with* him [cf 2.6]. 'Unto all pleasing' shows that the Christian's great interest in life must be to please his Lord in every respect. Although the word 'pleasing' denotes a cringing and subservient attitude in classical Greek, it has a favourable sense when transferred to the believer's relations to his Lord. 'To do anything to meet, to anticipate, His wishes, is not only the most beneficial but the most absolutely right thing we can do. It is His eternal and sacred due; it is at the same time the surest path to our own highest development and gain' (H. C. G. Moule).

bearing fruit in every good work, and increasing by the knowledge of God; (ASV margin) Paul further explains what is involved in this walk by a return to the image used in verse 6. In thus depicting the calling of believers in terms of the constant fruitfulness and growth effected by the true knowledge of God [*Deut* 32.2], the apostle implicitly condemns the barren intellectualism of the heretics who gloried in their 'superior' knowledge [2.8]. In the natural realm trees bear only one sort of fruit, but believers are expected to be fruitful 'in every good work' through the power of that divine seed which has been sown in their hearts. 'Unless, therefore, they produce every fruit, they do not answer the nature and efficacy of the seed. For *the fruit of the Spirit* is not one alone, but manifold; viz. *love, joy, peace, patience, longsuffering, goodness, benignity, and the like; Gal 5.22*' (Davenant).

*V*11: **strengthened with all power, according to the might of his glory, unto all patience and longsuffering with joy;**

Paul concludes his prayer for the Colossians by asking that they may be continually strengthened with all power, 'according to the might of his glory'. Lightfoot points out that 'glory' here stands for the power of God 'as *manifested* to men', and as the parallel passage in *Eph* 1.19, 20 indicates, this divine power was supremely manifested in the resurrection of Christ. Hence the request is that they may be empowered with the same might by which Christ was raised from the dead [cf *Rom* 6.4].

unto all patience and longsuffering with joy; 'Patience' is the brave endurance which triumphs over adverse circumstances, and 'longsuffering' is the capacity to endure the wrongs inflicted by others without being provoked to retaliation. The last words of the verse show that believers are not to meet these trials with Stoic fortitude or gloomy resignation, but are rather to receive them with Christian joy! [cf *v* 24; *Matt* 5.11; *James* 1.2f; 1 *Pet* 4.13].

*V*12: **giving thanks unto the Father, who made us meet to be partakers of the inheritance of the saints in light;**

This is so closely attached to the preceding prayer that at first sight it appears to be a continuation of it. But as Paul never concludes his prayers with thanksgiving, it is more likely that he here glides into a summons (taking 'giving thanks' as an imperative) to his readers to praise God for his saving grace in Christ [*vv* 12–14].

who has qualified you (NIV) By ascribing salvation solely to the action of God, Paul teaches us that it is not within the power of man to make himself fit to receive such a glorious inheritance [*Eph* 2.1–3]. He first brings down 'the pride of those, that give this glory to free will; boasting, that they have made themselves capable of salvation ... No, saith the apostle, This wholly appertaineth unto GOD. It is He, that hath made us capable. Of ourselves we cannot so much as think a good thought: so he affirms elsewhere' (Daillé). The aorist tense of the verb points to an instantaneous act which not only confers present grace [*v* 13], but also assures future glory [3.24]. The Old Testament colouring of this verse makes 'you' especially significant, for as Gentiles the Colossians might well thank God that they had been admitted to share in what had been the unique privilege of Jews ('the saints', i.e. Jewish believers: cf *Eph* 2.12, 13).

to share in the inheritance of the saints in the kingdom of light. (NIV) As each Israelite was assigned a portion of the promised land by lot, so every believer is given a share in the spiritual inheritance ('the kingdom of light') which that territorial possession prefigured [*Heb* 3.7–4.11]. 'In other words, the saints, possessed by Christ, themselves possess Christ as their riches and light, and are *qualified* to do so by the grace of the Father who gave the Son for them and to them. The reference is not immediately to the coming glory, but to the present grace' (H. C. G. Moule). [cf *v* 13; *Eph* 5.8] It should be noted that the Old Testament concept of the inheritance is here spiritualized and applied to the church as the new Israel of God [cf 1 *Pet* 2.9].

*V*13: **who delivered us out of the power of darkness, and translated us into the kingdom of the Son of his love;**

Paul now explains that we are qualified to share in this inheritance through what God accomplished in us by his converting grace, for it was then that he delivered us from the dominion of darkness and transferred us to the kingdom of his dear Son. Formerly, we were under the devil's authority, not merely as his helpless captives but also as his willing slaves [*Eph* 2.2]. Thus the misery of our plight by nature is here recalled to enhance our appreciation of the divine power which was put forth to secure our release from this bondage of death [*Is* 42.7; *Acts* 26.18]. The absolute nature of the apostle's antithesis shows that there is no middle state between the power of darkness and the kingdom of grace: 'all who breathe are either in the one or the other' (James Fergusson).

and translated us into the kingdom of the Son of his love; The same verb is used by Josephus of the Assyrian king Tiglath-Pileser, who transported the conquered inhabitants of Israel to his own kingdom. However, it is not our physical resettlement which Paul has in view, but our spiritual transfer to a present state of grace. 'For God is said to have translated us into the kingdom of his Son, because he hath communicated to us those spiritual gifts, and wrought in us that spiritual condition, which makes us subjects and members of Christ. Therefore, by the kingdom of Christ we must understand all the benefits of grace which are obtained through union with and subjection to Christ our spiritual King' (Davenant). As the phrase 'the Son of his love' points to Christ as the great object of God's love, this love of the Father for the Son thus becomes the pledge of his love for all who are 'in Christ' [*Eph* 1.6].

*V*14: **in whom we have our redemption, the forgiveness of our sins:** Here the liberation of an enslaved people is still in view, but the metaphor has changed from 'the victor who rescues the captive by force of arms [*v* 13] to the philanthropist who releases him by the payment of a ransom'

(Lightfoot). There can be no doubt that this is the idea conveyed by the word 'redemption', because the parallel verse in Ephesians spells out the price that was paid to secure our release [cf *Eph* 1.7: 'through his blood']. If the Colossian errorists had defined 'redemption' in terms of a mystic deliverance through the mere possession of superior knowledge this would explain Paul's insistence upon the *moral* content of the gospel, namely, that the primary blessing of God's great rescue by ransom is 'the forgiveness of sins'. As unforgiven sin presents an insuperable barrier to blessing, so the forgiveness of sins is the priceless boon which opens the door to every other spiritual blessing [*Rom* 4.6–8]. Although men may fondly claim that forgiveness is God's business, there can be no thought of 'cheap' forgiveness when we remember that our redemption cost God the life of his beloved Son. But we must not overlook the force of the all-important phrase 'in whom', which sets forth the condition of possessing this redemption. For we have the free forgiveness of our sins only as we are found in living union with Christ. 'We cannot get His gifts without Himself' (Maclaren).

*V*15: **who is the image of the invisible God, the firstborn of all creation; 16 for in him were all things created, in the heavens and upon the earth, things visible and things invisible, whether thrones or dominions or principalities or powers; all things have been created through him, and unto him; 17 and he is before all things, and in him all things consist. 18 And he is the head of the body, the church: who is the beginning, the firstborn from the dead; that in all things he might have the pre-eminence. 19 For it was the good pleasure *of the Father* that in him should all the fulness dwell; 20 and through him to reconcile all things unto himself, having made peace through the blood of his cross; through him,**

I say, **whether things upon the earth, or things in the heavens.**

The hymnic character of this passage has prompted much critical debate, and attempts have been made to show that a hymn emanating either from Hellenistic Judaism or Gnostic circles has been adapted by the author of Colossians for Christian use. But it is difficult to believe that one of the loftiest statements about Christ in the New Testament could have sprung from such a dubious background, especially when there is evidence to show that the apostle himself is the author of this 'cosmic' Christology. For it represents the logical development of the teaching which is already found in Paul's earlier letters (cf 1 *Cor* 8.6 for Christ's universal lordship: cf *Rom* 12.4f; 1 *Cor* 12.12, 13, 27 for the church as Christ's body). In this great outburst of praise Paul counters the unwarranted speculations of the Colossian heretics by affirming the pre-eminence of Christ in Creation [*vv* 15–17] and Redemption [*vv* 18–20].

who is the image of the invisible God, The word 'image' suggests both Representation and Manifestation (Lightfoot). The important point to note is that in ancient thought an 'image' was not regarded as a mere copy of the object it represented, for it was believed in some way to participate in the substance of that object. 'Image is not to be understood as a magnitude which is alien to the reality and present only in the consciousness. It has a share in the reality. Indeed, it is the reality' (H. Kleinknecht, *TDNT*, Vol. II, p. 389). Thus in Christ we see God fully revealed [*John* 14.9], because he alone is the perfect 'image' of 'the invisible God' [*v* 19; 2 *Cor* 4.4]. In other words, Christ's revelatory *function* rests upon his essential *relation* as the eternal Son of God [cf *Phil* 2.6]. But as the word 'image' also clearly recalls *Gen* 1.27, it may be asked

[29]

how Paul is able to relate this reference to man's creation 'in the image of God' to the pre-existent Son. According to Herman Ridderbos, the answer lies in the fact that Paul's preaching was necessarily determined by the 'redemptive-historical outlook' (*Paul – An Outline of His Theology*, p. 77). He nowhere separates Christ's Sonship from his Redeemership, because sinners may never consider what Christ is 'in himself' apart from what he is 'for them'. So it is through the redeeming work of Christ as the Last Adam [1 Cor 15.45] that the original purpose of God in creation is achieved and we see a renewal of the image of God in man [cf 3.10]. The apostle's thought therefore works back from the historical accomplishment of salvation to the eternal purpose which governed it.

the firstborn of all creation; The contention of the Arians and their successors in the sects today that Christ is here called a creature is refuted by the very wording 'the first-*born*' (rather than 'first-*created*'), and is certainly ruled out by the context [v 16]. The term 'firstborn' does not refer to temporal priority but to superiority of rank [cf Ps 89.27]. 'What is meant is the unique supremacy of Christ over all creatures as the Mediator of their creation' (W. Michaelis, *TDNT*, Vol. VI, p. 879). As then all things were created through Christ, he stands over against the entire creation as its rightful Lord and Heir [Heb 1.1, 2].

Although the designation of Christ as 'the firstborn of all creation' recalls Adam's dominion over the first creation [Gen 1.28ff], the parallel term 'the firstborn from the dead' [v 18] shows that Paul is describing Christ's 'primal' sovereignty over creation on the analogy of his significance as the Inaugurator of the new creation. Thus we find that this 'post-redemptive' perspective leads him to explain the meaning of Christ's work in categories which are derived from the first

Adam. Accordingly the crucial phrase 'the firstborn from the dead' means that the apostle sees Christ's resurrection as the pivotal event which secured the beginning of the new humanity, so that what was lost under the headship of Adam has now been regained by Christ in a far more glorious way. For the second Adam is the Son of God who has made his people the sharers of his divine life [1 *Cor* 15.45, 47], whereas the glory that Adam possessed as the 'image of God' and 'the firstborn of all creation' was but the finite reflection of Christ's essential glory as the eternal Son.

for in him were all things created, 'For' introduces the proof of the title given to the Son in the previous clause ('the firstborn of all creation'). Instead of the preposition 'through' which points to the agency of Christ in creation [see below and *John* 1.3; *Heb* 1.2], 'in' is used here to denote Christ as the 'sphere' in which creation took place. This is because Paul wishes to show 'that the conditioning cause of the act of creation resided in Him. The Eternal Word stood in the same relation to the created Universe as the Incarnate Christ to the Church' (T. K. Abbott). [cf 2.7, 10; *Rom* 8.1; 1 *Cor* 1.30; *Eph* 2.10] The definite historical act of creation is described by the aorist tense of the verb.

in the heavens and upon the earth, things visible and things invisible, An exhaustive enumeration which brings out the full meaning of 'all things', and thus indicates that the term admits of no exceptions. As therefore every created thing owes its very existence to Christ, it follows that nothing in the entire universe lies outside the scope of his sovereignty [*v* 17].

whether thrones or dominions or principalities or powers; By setting forth Christ as the Creator and Disposer of all spiritual powers, Paul implicitly condemns the false teaching at Colossae, which dethroned Christ from his supremacy by paying homage to angels [2.18]. In comparing this listing of angelic orders with that given in *Eph* 1.21, Lightfoot insists that no stress can be laid on the sequence of names, as though the apostle were formulating a precise doctrine of the celestial hierarchy. He clearly has no patience with this elaborate angelology, and brushes aside these speculations without remarking upon how much or how little truth there may be in them. 'The decisive point for Paul is that in no regard, whether as fate, or nature, or intermediate beings, or servants of God, can these powers either separate the Christian from Christ or lead him to Him' (W. Foerster, *TDNT*, Vol. II, p. 573).

all things have been created through him, and unto him;
The final clause presents Christ as the goal of all creation. The phrase 'in him' at the beginning of the verse represented Christ 'as the *conditional* cause of all things. All things came to pass within the sphere of His personality and as dependent upon it. Here He appears as the *mediating* cause; "through him" as in 1 *Cor* 8.6. "Unto him." All things, as they had their beginning in Him, tend *to Him* as their consummation, to depend on and serve Him' (Marvin Vincent). [cf *Heb* 2.10; *Rev* 22.13]

and he is before all things, and in him all things consist.
In this summarizing statement Paul reaffirms the absolute 'self-existence' of the eternal Son and declares him to be the Creator and Preserver of all things. The emphatic 'HE IS' recalls Christ's majestic claim, 'Before Abraham was, I AM' [*John* 8.58]. 'He who made all necessarily existed before all. Prior to His creative work, He had filled the unmeasured periods of an unbeginning eternity. Matter is not eternal ...

He pre-existed it, and called it into being. Everything is posterior to Him, and nothing coeval with Him' (John Eadie). But though the Son is independent of all things, all things must depend upon his sustaining power for their continued existence. 'He is the principle of cohesion in the universe. He impresses upon creation that unity and solidarity which makes it a cosmos instead of a chaos' (Lightfoot).

And he is the head of the body, the church: Having demonstrated Christ's sovereignty over creation, Paul next describes his pre-eminence in the church which is his new creation [*vv* 18-20]. 'And he' is repeated from the preceding verse to emphasize the fact that 'the Creator of the World is also the Head of the Church' (Lightfoot). By placing Christ's redemptive work within the context of his cosmic significance, Paul refutes the false teaching which assigned a reduced rôle to Christ in the economy of salvation and put the Colossians in danger of 'not holding fast the Head' [2.19]. Although the apostle here combines his familiar metaphor of the church as Christ's 'body' with the new concept of Christ as the 'head' of the church, it is important to note that even when they thus appear together both figures retain their independent meaning. 'When Paul writes that man is the head of the woman [1 *Cor* 11.3], he does not have in view the model of a single body of which the man is the head and the woman is the trunk. Paul goes on to say that Christ is the head of the man and that God is the "head" of Christ. When Paul asserts that the body grows up into the head and is nourished from the head [*Eph* 4.15, 16], we are not to seek for some physiological model relating the head to the rest of the body. Rather, Christ the head nourishes his body as a man nourishes and cherishes his wife, in a position of authority and primacy' (Edmund P. Clowney, *The Doctrine of the Church*, p. 45). This authority which Christ has over the church as its Head is grounded in the fact that the church owes its origin to him (just as the first woman came from man: cf 1 *Cor* 11.8), because Paul immediately adds that Christ is 'the beginning, the firstborn from the dead'. In other words, the figure of headship refers to the primacy which belongs to Christ as the source of the church's life, whereas the body metaphor shows that the church belongs to Christ as a wife belongs to her husband [*Eph* 5.28].

who is the beginning, the firstborn from the dead; Christ is called 'the beginning' because when he broke the bands of death, his resurrection also ensured that of his people [cf 1 *Cor* 15.20, 23]. As the One who rose in the power of an endless life, he is then 'the firstborn *from* the dead'. 'Only as he himself is one "from the dead" is Christ "firstborn". Only as he is part of that group which is (to be) raised does he enjoy this exalted status' (Richard B. Gaffin, *The Centrality of the Resurrection*, p. 38). This stands in pointed contrast to *v* 16, for while the eternal Son is the Lord of all creation by divine right, he attained the lordship of the church only through the redemptive travail of the cross and the triumph of the resurrection [*Rom* 1.4].

that in all things he might have the pre-eminence. Or more literally, 'that in all things he alone might become pre-eminent'. 'As He *is* first with respect to the Universe, so it was ordained that He should *become* first with respect to the Church as well ... The relation between Christ's headship of the Universe by virtue of His Eternal Godhead and His headship of the Church by virtue of His Incarnation and Passion and Resurrection is somewhat similarly represented in *Phil* 2.6 sq. *existing in the form of God ... taking the form of a servant ... becoming obedient unto death ... wherefore also God highly exalted him*' (Lightfoot).

For it was the good pleasure *of the Father* **that in him should all the fulness dwell;** This pre-eminence belongs to Christ because it was God's 'good pleasure' [*Luke* 2.14] 'that all the fulness should take up its abode in him' [cf *John* 1.14, 16]. Many commentators suggest that 'fulness' was a catchword of the Colossian heretics which Paul here takes up in order to refute their teaching, but the non-Gnostic use of the same word in Ephesians makes this unlikely (see further R. P. Martin's article 'Fulness' in *The New Bible Dictionary*, p. 442). As John Murray observes, this verse cannot mean that it was the Father's will that fulness of Deity should dwell in the Son [*John* 1.1, 2]. Hence this fulness must be regarded as the fulness which belongs to Christ as the Word made flesh for our salvation. The fact that *Col* 2.9 refers to Christ's essential Godhood is not incompatible with this conclusion, for the fulness that Christ possesses as the eternal Son does not interfere with 'the fulness he comes to possess for the execution of messianic office'. Moreover, the analogy of Paul's teaching in *Eph* 1.23 'would point to the conclusion that the church is the fulness of Christ, because to the church as the body of Christ is being imparted the fulness that is in Christ. The church is the recipient of that fulness of righteousness, wisdom, knowledge, power, grace, goodness, patience, love, truth, and mercy, which has its permanent abode in Christ, and abides in him in terms of an economy that has no relevance apart from the purpose and realization of this same communication. This fulness believers do not receive as discrete individuals, but in the unity and fellowship of the church as the body of Christ' (*Collected Writings of John Murray*, Vol. II, pp. 301–4).

and through him to reconcile all things unto himself, having made peace through the blood of his cross; through him, *I say*, **whether things upon the earth, or things in the heavens.** It was also God's good pleasure to reconcile all things to himself through Christ, whose sacrificial death on the cross was the means by which this peace was secured. Paul clearly underlines the cosmic sweep of Christ's reconciling work by his insistence upon the inclusive scope of 'all things'. As all creation was involved in the consequences of man's sin, so the reconciliation effected by Christ encompasses the whole universe [*Rom* 8.20ff; *Eph* 1.10]. But the final restoration of 'all things' may not be equated with the salvation of 'all beings', for Paul later shows that this 'reconciliation' was only achieved through Christ's conquest of the demonic powers which had introduced the discordant principle of sin into God's world [2.15]. The relevance of the apostle's statement for the Colossians is well explained by William Hendriksen: *Through Christ and his cross the universe is brought back or restored to its proper relationship to God in the sense that as a just reward for his obedience Christ was exalted to the Father's right hand, from which position of authority and power he rules the entire universe in the interest of the church and to the glory of God* [cf 2.10].

*V*21: **And you, being in time past alienated and enemies in your mind in your evil works, 22. yet now hath he reconciled in the body of his flesh through death, to present you holy and without blemish and unreprovable before him:**

As those who were once pagan Gentiles, the Colossians are here exhorted to remember with gratitude what Christ's grace has accomplished in delivering them from their former servitude to sin [*Eph* 2.11, 12]. For when they were thus estranged from God, the hostility of their minds found its natural expression in their evil deeds [*Eph* 2.2f; 4.18]. 'The apostle charges them not merely with spiritual and latent

[36]

hostility to God, but with the manifestation of that hostility in open acts of unnatural rebellion' (Eadie).

yet now hath he reconciled in the body of his flesh through death, That Christ is the subject of the sentence is shown by the unusual expression 'the body of his flesh through (his) death', which is evidently directed against those who taught that angelic intermediaries assisted in the work of reconciliation. In opposing this speculation Paul emphasizes the fact that it was by the putting to death of this body of flesh that reconciliation was achieved, and thereby excludes these spiritual powers from any part in the work of salvation [cf *Heb* 2.14ff].

to present you holy and without blemish and unreprovable before him: Christ's purpose in submitting to the death of the cross was that he might present before himself in glory a people who are so consecrated and cleansed as to be without blemish and above reproach [cf *Eph* 5.27; 2 *Cor* 11.2]. Lightfoot (who prefers another construction which makes God the subject of the sentence) gives a *sacrificial* meaning to the verb in his paraphrase: 'He will present you a living sacrifice, an acceptable offering unto Himself.' In rejecting this interpretation, Abbott points out that the meaning of 'to present' is here determined by the *judicial* term 'unreprovable', and rightly observes: 'May we not add that the thought expressed in Lightfoot's paraphrase has no parallel in the N.T.? For *Rom* 12.1 does not support the idea of God presenting believers to Himself as a sacrifice.'

*V*23: **if so be that ye continue in the faith, grounded and steadfast, and not moved away from the hope of the gospel which ye heard, which was preached in all**

creation under heaven; whereof I Paul was made a minister.

The reality of the Colossians' interest in the reconciliation wrought by Christ will be evidenced by their continuance in the faith. For though Paul assumes that they will so persevere, the presence of false teachers in their midst inevitably puts a question mark against their fidelity, hence his cautionary 'if indeed' (cf *v* 28). Since salvation is through faith in Christ, this is the foundation on which they must build to find true stability, for there is no other way of avoiding the peril of constantly shifting from the sure hope held out by the gospel [*Matt* 7.24–27].

which ye heard, which was preached in all creation under heaven; whereof I Paul was made a minister. Here three points are made to stress the importance of continuing in the faith. 1. The gospel they had heard from Epaphras was the means of their conversion [*v* 7]. 2. As the same gospel had been proclaimed throughout the world, this universality points to its authenticity [*v* 6]. Paul's expression probably means that the good news had reached all the important cities of the Empire and was spreading from these centres to the provinces (as the province of Asia was evangelized from Ephesus: cf *Rom* 15.19–23). 3. Paul declares that he was made a minister of the gospel. It is not for the purpose of magnifying his office that Paul makes this claim, but to impress on the Colossians that the gospel which they had heard from Epaphras, and which was proclaimed in all the world, was the selfsame gospel that he preached.

*V*24: **Now I rejoice in my sufferings for your sake, and fill up on my part that which is lacking of the afflictions**

of Christ in my flesh for his body's sake, which is the church;

From the remembrance of his call to the ministry Paul returns to the 'now' of his present sufferings as 'the prisoner of Christ Jesus in behalf of you Gentiles' [*Eph* 3.1]. As Christ's apostle he rejoices in these sufferings, for what he endures in his own person ('in my flesh') is for the benefit of the church ('for his body's sake'), since he is thus filling up what is lacking in 'the afflictions of Christ'. This remarkable expression obviously cannot mean that the atoning sacrifice of Christ on the cross was incomplete and needed to be supplemented by the sufferings of his apostle [cf 2.13f]. Moreover, the term 'afflictions' never occurs in the New Testament in connection with the *personal* sufferings of Christ. Paul is speaking rather of his participation in the afflictions of the *corporate* Christ. Such are the afflictions which the glorified Christ reckons as his own because his people bear them for his sake [*Acts* 9.4, 5]. These tribulations are the lot of the believing community on earth [*Acts* 14.22; 1 *Thess* 3.3], for the confession of Christ before men inevitably attracts a share of the same hatred which reached its climax in his crucifixion [*Heb* 13.13]. And as the tale of 'Messianic woes' must be fulfilled before the end of the age [*Mark* 13.5–27], Paul rejoices in his exceptional vocation of suffering on behalf of the church [*Acts* 9.16], because it serves to bring nearer the new age of glory which Christ will inaugurate at his return [3.4].

*V*25: **whereof I was made a minister, according to the dispensation of God which was given me to you-ward, to fulfil the word of God,**

In verse 23 Paul spoke of himself as a minister of the gospel, and now he reminds the Colossians of the divine commission which made him a minister of the church at large [*v* 24], in case they were tempted to think that their spiritual welfare lay outside the range of his ministry [2.1]. He exercises this ministry towards them in accordance with the 'stewardship' (ASV margin) that has been entrusted to him by God. For though he *serves* men as their minister, he only engages in this service because he has been *appointed* to it by God [cf 1 *Cor* 4.1, 2; 9.17]. Consequently the steward has no power 'to do any thing of his own head, and after his own phantasy; but only to dispense, what the Master hath given him; and precisely in such manner, as he hath prescribed him' (Daillé). Although some take the phrase 'to fulfil the word of God' to refer to the geographical extension of the gospel (as in *v* 23), it is more likely that Paul has in view the universal scope of his commission as the apostle to the Gentiles. His task was 'to fill up the full measure of the Gospel, both in its reception by the Gentiles [*v* 27a] and in the moral and spiritual completion of every believer [*v* 28]. He toils and contends for nothing less [*v* 29]' (A. Lukyn Williams).

*V*26: *even* **the mystery which hath been hid for ages and generations: but now hath it been manifested to his saints,**

In this verse the message entrusted to the apostle is more precisely designated by the term 'mystery'. Lightfoot thought that Paul borrowed the word from the heathen mysteries in order to point a contrast between those secret rites and the gospel which is offered to all. But the fact that the singular ('the mystery') is not used in connection with these pagan cults tells against this assumption, as does the appearance of the term in Paul's earlier Epistles [*Rom* 16.25–7; 1 *Cor* 2.6–10]. The gospel 'mystery' is not an unexplained riddle, but a divine secret which, though proclaimed to all, is understood only by those whom the Spirit of God savingly enlightens [*Mark* 4.11; 1 *Cor* 2.9f]. Thus God's plan of salvation for Jews *and* Gentiles [cf *Eph* 3.3–9], which has been hidden for ages and generations, is *now* revealed to 'his saints', i.e. to *all* believers. 'It came upon the world as a sudden surprise. The moment of its revelation was the moment of its fulfilment' (Lightfoot).

*V*27: **to whom God was pleased to make known what is the riches of the glory of this mystery among the Gentiles, which is Christ in you, the hope of glory:**

to whom God willed to make known It was the will of God to make known the mystery to the saints. 'Willed' stands first in the Greek for emphasis. 'The revelation was so momentous in its issue, so signal in its method, and so contrary to human foresight and prejudice, that it proceeded evidently from "the will of God" . . . "Who was I", said Peter, "that I could withstand God?" [*Acts* 11.17]. The Ephesian letter delights to dwell on *God's will* as the cause of the whole counsel and work of salvation' (G. G. Findlay).

what is the riches of the glory of this mystery among the Gentiles, Paul struggles with the limitations of language as he attempts to give adequate expression to the munificence of God's grace. How great are the riches of the divine glory thus outpoured in the revelation of this mystery among the Gentiles! It was in the conversion of the Gentiles that this wealth was fully displayed, 'for it overflowed all barriers of caste or race. Judaism was "beggarly" [*Gal* 4.9] in comparison, since its treasures sufficed only for a few' (Lightfoot).

which is Christ in you, the hope of glory: Some prefer 'Christ *among* you', but what is evidently intended to be the climactic statement would be a distinct anti-climax if it referred to nothing more than the beginning of the Gentile mission. 'Christ *in* you Gentiles!' – 'that is the great surprise. None could have foreseen or imagined it. It was God's secret. He has disclosed it to us' (J. Armitage Robinson). The aspect of the mystery revealed in Ephesians concerns the admission of the Gentiles as fellow-heirs with Jewish believers, whereas here Paul stresses their wonderful privilege in knowing the power of the indwelling Christ, whose presence within their hearts constitutes the pledge of future glory [cf *Rom* 8.10].

*V*28: **whom we proclaim, admonishing every man and teaching every man in all wisdom, that we may present every man perfect in Christ;**

whom we proclaim, In contrast to the false teachers, *we* (i.e. Paul and his fellow evangelists including Epaphras) proclaim Christ! 'Proclaim' belongs to 'the language of mission', but as that involves 'declaring the unique historical reality of Jesus', this word must also be one of 'instruction, admonition and tradition' (J. Schniewind, *TDNT*, Vol. I, pp. 71–72). And since the apostolic proclamation of the gospel presented Christ as the only Saviour [*Acts* 4.12], 'they only preach Christ aright and as they ought to do, who teach that all hope of salvation for mankind is laid up in him alone, and who acknowledge that we receive the riches of divine grace through him alone ... He who makes Christ a sort of halfway Saviour and Mediator, does not in fact preach him, but the chimera of his own brain' (Davenant).

admonishing every man and teaching every man in all wisdom, The preaching of Christ is effected through admonition and teaching. Although this dual ministry is seen as the task of the whole community in 3.16, it is primarily the function of the apostle to warn against error and to teach the truth [*Acts* 20.31; 1 *Cor* 4.17]. The phrase 'in all wisdom' probably points to the manner of the teaching rather than its content. The thrice-repeated 'every man' emphasizes the universality of Paul's gospel [3.11], 'in opposition to the doctrine of an intellectual exclusiveness taught by the false teachers' (Abbott).

that we may present every man perfect in Christ; This is the ultimate object of the apostle's preaching. The word 'perfect' can scarcely mean that he intended to make every man an 'initiate' of the gospel mystery; it rather expresses his desire that every man might so grow to full maturity in Christ as to appear before God without confusion in the day of judgment [cf *Eph* 4.13]. The universality of Paul's aim is in perfect accord with the *revealed* will of God (as opposed to his *secret* decree: *Deut* 29.29), and is therefore an example for all preachers [1 *Tim* 2.4]. For what 'God himself hath declared to be his will in offering the Gospel, the same also ought to be the will of his Ministers in preaching it' (Davenant).

*V*29: **whereunto I labour also, striving according to his working, which worketh in me mightily.**

With this great end in view (*v* 28), Paul toils to the point of weariness, struggling with intense exertion by means of Christ's supernatural power which works in him mightily. The imprisoned apostle employs this athletic metaphor [1 *Tim* 4.10] to describe the constant spiritual conflict in which he is engaged on behalf of all the churches [*v* 24; 2.1]. But though the striving is Paul's, the effectiveness of his labours is entirely due to Christ's power. As Findlay well says, 'Never do we find this consciousness of the Divine power dwelling in himself expressed by Paul with such joyous confidence as at this period' [cf *Phil* 4.13; *Eph* 3.7, 20).

CHAPTER TWO

Although Paul was personally unknown to the believers at Colossae and Laodicea, he strives that they may be so confirmed in their faith in Christ as to give no heed to the novel doctrines of the false teachers [vv 1–7]. Such specious philosophy is after the rudiments of the world and not after Christ. It is because they are already complete in Christ, in whom dwells all the fulness of the Godhead, that they must not worship the angelic powers which are subject to his lordship [vv 8–10]. They need no circumcision of the flesh, for in Christ they have received the true circumcision of the spirit. Their baptism had set forth this rising to new life, received from God through Christ's finished work, by which the bond that stood against them was abolished and the defeat of all hostile powers secured [vv 11–15]. It is therefore folly to observe ritual ordinances, which were but a shadow of Christ, when they are now in possession of the reality [vv 16, 17]. The worship of angels, though urged as an exercise in humility, is rather the fruit of carnal pride, because it denies Christ's sole primacy as the Head and Sustainer of his church [vv 18, 19]. If they died with Christ to the mere ideas of men, they must renounce the ascetic practices of human devising which flatter pride, and thus serve only to indulge the flesh instead of mortifying it [vv 20–23].

VI: **For I would have you know how greatly I strive for you, and for them at Laodicea, and for as many as have not seen my face in the flesh;**

In approaching the purpose of the letter, Paul acquaints his readers with the strife in which he is engaged on their behalf, in order to establish a personal bond with the Christians in the cities of the Lycus valley whom he has never met [4.16]. This conflict is not beyond the bounds of his commission, for as the apostle to the Gentiles, his interest is not limited to the churches of his own founding, but extends to the believers in every community of which he has no first-hand knowledge [cf *Rom* 1.13]. 'His prison cell was like the focus of some reverberating gallery in which every whisper spoken all round the circumference was heard and the heart that was held captive there was set vibrating in all its chords by every sound from any of the Churches' (Maclaren).

*V*2: **that their hearts may be comforted, they being knit together in love, and unto all riches of the full assurance of understanding, that they may know the mystery of God, *even* Christ, 3 in whom are all the treasures of wisdom and knowledge hidden.**

This expresses the purpose for which Paul strives in prayer: It is that they may be strengthened in heart and welded together in love, and thus attain to the full wealth of that assured understanding, which will result in a true knowledge of the mystery of God, namely, Christ. 'Strengthened' is preferable to 'comforted', for the false teaching which threatened the faith of Paul's readers meant that they needed something more than comfort. 'It was not consolation that was required, but confirmation in the right faith' (Abbott). The importance of the place here assigned to love in the attainment of spiritual understanding should be noted (cf *Eph* 3.17f and 3.14 where the Colossians are urged to put on love, 'the bond of perfection'). 'As against all those who tried

[46]

to intellectualize the Christian faith, speaking of knowledge (*gnosis*) as if it were an end in itself, Paul emphasizes that the revelation of God cannot be properly known apart from the cultivation of brotherly love within the Christian community' (F. F. Bruce). The experience of being united in love will bring them the spiritual wealth that consists in the complete insight into God's mystery – Christ, who is the very embodiment of the divine wisdom [cf *v* 9 and see comment on 1.26].

in whom are all the treasures of wisdom and knowledge hidden. It is probably with a sidelong glance at the rival claims made for angelic intermediaries by the heretics that Paul presents Christ as the sole repository of 'all the treasures of wisdom and knowledge'. The terms 'wisdom' and 'knowledge' also occur together in *Rom* 11.33 where they describe the character of God as this is revealed in the great drama of redemption, and the fact that here they are virtually fused together by the use of one definite article is perhaps a warning against making subtle distinctions between them. The divine wisdom differs from the derived wisdom of men in that it is original and creative. Paul's attribution of this wisdom to Christ means that he is the personal fulfilment of 'all that the Wisdom of God was, according to the Wisdom Literature, and more still' (C. F. D. Moule). [cf *Prov* 8. 22ff] For Christ is not only the Creator and Preserver of all things [1.16, 17], but he is also the perfect Revealer of God and the one Redeemer of men [1.15, 20]. 'Hidden' does not mean kept concealed, but stored up as in a treasure chest. 'The treasures of wisdom are hid, not from us, but for us, in Christ. They who would be wise and knowing, must apply themselves to Christ. We must spend upon the stock which is laid up for us in him, and draw from the treasures which are hid in him. He is the *Wisdom of God*, and is *of God made unto us Wisdom*, &c. 1 *Cor* 1.24, 30' (Matthew Henry).

*V*4: **This I say, that no one may delude you with persuasiveness of speech.**

In his first direct reference to the false teachers, Paul warns of the danger of being deluded by their 'plausible (but false) arguments' (Arndt-Gingrich). 'Under this word the Apostle comprehends rhetorical and flattering insinuations, sophistical and intricate subtleties; with which they endeavoured either to insinuate or force an entrance into the minds of men. In short; whatever is so flattering to human reason, by its specious colouring, as to lead a man from Christ, is to be referred to the pernicious *enticing words*. This deceitful sophistry the Apostle condemns in 1 *Cor* 2.4. Not that *persuasiveness of words* is in itself condemnable, for it is a great excellence of speech; but the abuse of it, when it acts by apparent, but false reasons, and is employed to impose upon men' (Davenant).

*V*5: **For though I am absent in the flesh, yet am I with you in the spirit, joying and beholding your order, and the steadfastness of your faith in Christ.**

For though absent in body, I am with you in spirit, and rejoice to see your orderly array and the firm front which your faith in Christ presents. (NEB) Although Paul's imprisonment prevents him from dealing with this menacing situation in person, he assures his readers that he is with them in spirit, and like a general reviewing his troops before the battle, he is confident that their faith in Christ will enable them to maintain 'good order' and 'closed ranks' in the face of the enemy. 'See how by praising them he doth oblige them to regard his advertisements; and by the very consideration of their having so well begun, doth more and more engage them to holy persevering to the end' (Daillé).

V6: **As therefore ye received Christ Jesus the Lord, *so* walk in him, 7 rooted and builded up in him, and established in your faith, even as ye were taught, abounding in thanksgiving.**

As therefore ye received Christ Jesus as Lord, Paul now exhorts the community to continue in the faith they had 'received' through the ministry of Epaphras [1.7]. This is the technical word for accepting what is handed on by oral tradition [1 *Cor* 11.23; 15.3], but the tradition here is not merely the doctrine about Christ, for Christ himself is identified with the gospel [cf *Eph* 4.20]. Paul represents Christ, rather than the gospel, as the object of instruction, 'because the central point in the Colossian heresy was the subversion of the true idea of the Christ' (Lightfoot). For in believing the testimony given to Christ Jesus, they had received him *as Lord*, and so were bound to be obedient to him alone [1.10].

continue to walk in him, As there could be no walking in Christ without a prior reception of him, so this 'ability to walk is the result of communicated animation' (Eadie). In other words, the power to live a new life depends upon daily communion with the living Lord. Thus Christ must be 'the encompassing and guiding and controlling element of every step of life' (J. A. Beet).

having been rooted, and being built up in him, As usual the richness of Paul's thought leads to the mixing of his metaphors. In the first metaphor Christ is regarded as the soil in which they have been rooted, while in the second he is viewed as the cohesive element in the ensuing process of being built up in the faith. With regard to the first, Daillé points out that those who are rooted in Christ can never be plucked up by any effort, however violent it may be. The winds of false doctrine leave them unmoved, because the sweet sap which they draw from Christ, 'as from a rich soil, doth content them, and purgeth them of that foolish and childish itching humour, which openeth the ears of the weak and unstable to such things. But if you be not thus rooted in CHRIST, it will be no great difficulty to pluck you from the station you are in.'

and being established in the faith, even as ye were taught, To become established in the faith is to continue in the teaching of their faithful pastor Epaphras. Far from interfering with the work of an honoured colleague, Paul places the whole weight of his apostolic authority behind it [1.23].

abounding in thanksgiving. As thanksgiving is the hallmark of spiritual life, so ingratitude always points to a slight appreciation of gospel grace. This probably accounts for the sustained emphasis upon thanksgiving in Colossians, for only those who fail to realize the fulness of Christ seek some further satisfaction outside of him [v 10]. A. Lukyn Williams also suggests that there may be an intentional contrast here between the Christian's thanksgiving over everything [3.17] and 'the lack of liberty to be found in the false teaching, vv 16, 21'. [cf 1 Tim 4.3, 4]

*V*8: **Take heed lest there shall be any one that maketh spoil of you through his philosophy and vain deceit, after the tradition of men, after the rudiments of the world, and not after Christ:**

Paul now warns the Colossians to be on their guard, for they were in danger of being kidnapped by the false teachers! The word 'maketh spoil', meaning *to carry off as booty* or *as a captive*, is here used 'figuratively of carrying someone away from the truth into the slavery of error' (Arndt-Gingrich). If they would avoid this bondage, they must reject that teaching which the preachers of error dignified by the term 'philosophy', and which Paul roundly condemns for its 'vain deceit'. He goes on to expose the true character of this deceptive system in three descriptive phrases: 1. It is 'after the tradition of men'. In contrast to the *divine* origin of the gospel 'tradition' [*v* 6], this dogma could not be traced to any higher source than 'the tradition *of men*' [*v* 22]. 2. It is 'after the rudiments of the world'. What originates in men clearly cannot transcend the world, and it is therefore futile to seek salvation by the fleshly wisdom that relies upon those rules and regulations which belong to a perishing order. On the much disputed meaning of this phrase see the further comment on verse 20. 3. It is 'not after Christ'. Contrary to the superior claims put forward by the errorists, Paul affirms that their specious reasoning is not in accord with the truth which God has fully revealed in Christ. Every heresy is marked by the failure to conform to this God-given standard.

*V*9: **for in him dwelleth all the fulness of the Godhead bodily,**

As Eadie observes, Any 'philosophy' not 'after Christ' must be earthly and delusive. It has missed the central truth, 'for in him dwells all the fulness of the Godhead bodily'. Here the term 'the fulness' [see comment on 1.19] is defined by the phrase 'of the Godhead' and the mode of its manifestation is explained by the word 'bodily'. In *Rom* 1.20 Paul speaks of the 'divinity' of God in reference to the divine qualities which are revealed in the creation; whereas he uses the stronger word, 'Godhead', to show that in Christ there dwells all the fulness of absolute Deity: 'not merely the Divine attributes, but the

Divine nature itself' (Bengel). Of the many interpretations of 'bodily', the literal is the most natural [cf *John* 1.14]. 'It is because the fulness took on some visible form in Christ that it became knowable to man. It is worth noting that the verb is in the present tense which points to the continuing effect of the incarnation as an act of revelation' (Donald Guthrie).

*V*10: **and in him ye are made full, who is the head of all principality and power:**

This great Christological statement leads directly to the practical conclusion which the Colossians are to draw from it. Since they have been made full 'in him', they must not seek by supplementary rites and beliefs the 'completeness' they already possess in Christ alone [*vv* 11, 17ff]. 'We are declared to be complete not *from him*, or *by him* only, but *in him* ... There is no necessity that they who wish to drink of a fountain should enter the fountain itself; because, standing without that, they may draw from thence to quench their thirst: but it is not so with Christ, who is the fountain of grace and righteousness to us, for we cannot receive of his fulness unless we are in him' (Davenant).

who is the head of all principality and power: This is added to convince them of the futility of invoking angelic powers when these are all subject to the supreme lordship of Christ. But though Christ is described as their 'head', it should be noted that they are not called his 'body', for the special intimacy of that relationship is reserved for Christ's people [1.18].

*V*11: **in whom ye were also circumcised with a circumcision not made with hands, in the putting off of the body**

of the flesh, in the circumcision of Christ; 12 having been buried with him in baptism, wherein ye were also raised with him through faith in the working of God, who raised him from the dead. 13 And you, being dead through your trespasses and the uncircumcision of your flesh, you, *I say*, did he make alive together with him, having forgiven us all our trespasses; 14 having blotted out the bond written in ordinances that was against us, which was contrary to us: and he hath taken it out of the way, nailing it to the cross; 15 having despoiled the principalities and the powers, he made a show of them openly, triumphing over them in it.

In describing the 'fulness' given by God to the Colossians 'in Christ' [*v* 10], Paul lays stress on three things: 1. The spiritual circumcision which was set forth in their baptism; 2. The reality of their participation in Christ's resurrection life; 3. The significance of Christ's triumph over all the powers of evil.

in whom ye were also circumcised with a circumcision not made with hands, This unexpected reference to circumcision suggests that Paul is replying to the claims made for it by the false teachers. But in contrast to the Jewish legalists who made circumcision a condition of salvation [*Acts* 15.1], these 'free thinkers' presumably had their own reasons for recommending it. Possibly they regarded it as a prophylactic against the sins of the flesh [*v* 23], as a protection against the power of evil spirits [*v* 15], or as the badge of their assumed superiority. But whatever arguments were used to persuade the Colossians to be circumcised, at least it is clear that Paul here cuts the ground from under them, for he assures his Gentile readers that 'in Christ' they were already the recipients of that 'spiritual' circumcision which was 'not

[53]

made with hands' [cf *Rom* 2.29]. The aorist tense points to the time of their conversion and reception into the church by baptism [*v* 12].

in the putting off of the body of the flesh, in the circumcision of Christ; Whereas circumcision was a minor physical operation which removed only a portion of the body, in spiritual circumcision 'the whole corrupt, carnal nature is put away like a garment which is taken off and laid aside' (Vincent). [3.9; *Rom* 6.6] 'The circumcision of Christ' is the circumcision that belongs to Christ, and is effected through union with him, in contrast to the circumcision of Moses. It is important to note that in this passage the rite of circumcision is not likened to Christian baptism, but contrasted with it.

having been buried with him in baptism, wherein ye were also raised with him through faith in the working of God, who raised him from the dead. According to the (pre-Pauline) practice of the Early Church, baptism was not only the funeral of the old life, but also the beginning of an entirely new life [*Rom* 6.3ff]. 'They were, in fact, "buried" with Christ when they were plunged in the baptismal water, in token that they had died so far as their old life of sin was concerned; they were raised again with Christ when they emerged from the water, in token that they had received a new life, which was nothing less than participation in Christ's own resurrection life' (F. F. Bruce, *Romans*, p. 136). But this union with Christ, of which the baptismal act was the outward and visible sign, was only experienced through personal faith 'in the working of God' [cf *Rom* 4.24; 6.8; 10.9]. 'Faith is the subjective means by which the grace is received; only by a belief in the resurrection can the rising again with Christ be appropriated by the individual. By belief in the resurrection of Christ we believe in the power of God, of which it is an

[54]

evidence; and this belief, again, is the means by which that power works in the life and produces an effect analogous to that resurrection' (Abbott).

And you, being dead through your trespasses and the uncircumcision of your flesh, you, *I say*, did he make alive together with him, having forgiven us all our trespasses; 'And you' means 'you as well as Christ', for God who raised Christ from the dead also raised you from the sepulchre of your sins when he quickened you with Christ. As Gentiles, the Colossians had been doubly dead 'through [= by reason of] trespasses' and the 'uncircumcision' of their flesh. They were not only cut off from the life of God by their sins, but their physical condition was then [but not now: cf *Eph* 2.11, 12] the true symbol of their unprivileged state as those who lay outside the scope of God's covenant mercy. 'Having forgiven' and 'having blotted out' (in the following clause) are both coincident aorist participles. The first shows that the forgiveness was contemporary with God's quickening grace in conversion, while the second specifies the act by which this comprehensive pardon was secured [*v* 14]. As Paul here comes to the heart of Christian experience, he includes himself with all believers ('us'). He is 'eager to claim his share in the transgression, that he may claim it also in the forgiveness' (Lightfoot).

having blotted out the bond that was against us by its ordinances: (ASV margin) Paul now explains how God was able to forgive us all our trespasses: He wiped out the bond which testified against us by means of its unfulfilled demands. Here the figure of a 'bond' is used by the apostle to illustrate the condemning power of the law. The bond was a statement of indebtedness, an IOU signed by the debtor (see *Phil* 19 for an example of the form). Conscience forces all men to sign this bond, to acknowledge their disobedience to God's revealed will: for the Jew has broken the written law, and the Gentile has not followed the dictates of his heart [Rom 2.15]. But just as writing could be washed off the surface of papyrus because ancient ink contained no acid, so God in his mercy has completely erased the record that stood against us. For on the cross Christ took this bond of sin and condemnation and discharged the debt by exhausting the penalty on our behalf [cf Gal 3.13; 2 Cor 5.21].

and he hath taken it out of the way, nailing it to the cross; Although God is clearly the subject from verse 13, at this point Paul appears to switch his thought to Christ [vv 14b, 15]. This change of subject is suggested by the change in construction, which shows that the bond of indictment against us has been permanently removed by Christ. The phrase that follows explains the way in which Christ rid us of the bond: 'nailing it to the cross'. Paul is probably alluding to the Roman practice of putting a notice over the cross of a crucified man to set forth the crime for which he was condemned. But though the charge under which Christ died was that of claiming to be 'The King of the Jews' [Mark 15.26], Paul boldly hails Christ's willing sacrifice as the great victory that forever removed the sentence of death which the law justly pronounced against us [Gal 3.13].

having despoiled the principalities and the powers, he made a show of them openly, triumphing over them in it. The situation in Colossae leads Paul to depict Christ's death on the cross as the decisive triumph over all the demonic powers of evil, for the false teaching which exalted angels at the expense of Christ clearly owed its inspiration to these defeated powers. 'In it' refers to the cross, where Christ turned apparent defeat into the conquest which disarmed

Satan's hosts of their power to retain the spoils [*Luke* 11.22]. 'The paradox of the crucifixion is thus placed in the strongest light – triumph in helplessness and glory in shame. The convict's gibbet is the victor's car' (Lightfoot). As therefore only Christ is Lord, the good angels cannot lead the Colossians to God [1 *Tim* 2.5], and the bad angels cannot separate them from God [*Rom* 8.38, 39]. There is but one message of hope that can relieve modern man of his frustration and despair. 'Christ crucified and risen is Lord of all; all the forces of the universe are subject to Him, not only the benign ones but the hostile ones as well. They are all subject to Him as their Creator; the latter are subject to Him also as their Conqueror. And therefore to be united to Him is to be liberated from their thraldom, to enjoy perfect freedom, to overcome all the power of evil because Christ's victory is ours' (F. F. Bruce). [cf *Eph* 6.10–18].

*V*16: **Let no man therefore judge you in meat, or in drink, or in respect of a feast day or a new moon or a sabbath day: 17 which are a shadow of the things to come; but the body is Christ's.**

Since Christ has gained the victory over all hostile powers and is the sovereign Lord of the universe, the Colossians must not capitulate to the false teachers whose rigid demands were presumably designed to please the angelic mediators they worshipped [*v* 18]. They must let no one take them to task in the matter of eating and drinking. The error in view is not the adoption of Jewish food laws (which in any case had little to say about drink), but the ascetic abstention which was influenced by pagan thought and practice. For in the ancient world it was believed that fasting made men receptive to ecstatic revelations from the gods. However, the reference to the observance of annual ('feast day'), monthly ('new moon'), and weekly ('sabbath day') holy days here points to the Judaistic element in this syncretistic 'heresy'. These are dismissed by Paul as 'a shadow of the things to come', because the Mosaic ritual is superseded by the arrival of 'the body' it served for a time to represent [cf *Heb* 10.1]. Thus instead of contrasting the *shadow* with the *substance*, Paul again emphasizes the term 'body', which refers to the church as Christ's body. The body belongs to Christ, for spiritual reality is only found in living communion with the Lord, and this discloses the supreme folly of 'not holding fast the Head' [*v* 19].

*V*18: **Let no man rob you of your prize by a voluntary humility and worshipping of the angels, dwelling in the things which he hath seen, vainly puffed up by his fleshly mind,**

Let no one disqualify you by taking pleasure in humility and the worship of angels, Our difficulty in grasping the meaning of what the Colossians must have understood is probably due to Paul's ironical quotation of catchwords used by the false teachers. These men took pleasure in the self-imposed 'humility' of an asceticism [*v* 23] which no doubt included the fasting that prepared them to receive their ecstatic visions (see next clause and comment on *v* 16). In contrast to such carnal 'humility' which involves scorn for those who do not participate in this mortification of the body, Paul urges them to put on the true humility [3.12] that characterizes the new man in Christ (so W. Grundmann, *TDNT*, Vol. VIII, p. 22). The heretics further flaunted this spirit of false humility in the worship of angels, for they claimed a superior reverence for God by insisting that he could only be approached through a host of angelic mediators. This was the 'Gnostic' element in the Colossian heresy. It assumed 'that humanity, debased by the contact with matter,

must reach after God through successive grades of intermediate beings' (Vincent).

taking his stand upon the things which he hath seen,
(ASV margin) The discovery of a second-century inscription
in the temple of Apollo at Klaros has thrown light on this
puzzling phrase. It refers to someone, who having undergone
the rite of initiation, 'entered into' the inner sanctuary, thus
'*taking his stand on what he has seen* in the mysteries' (Arndt-
Gingrich). This coincidence of language probably points to a
form of incipient Gnosticism in Colossae which anticipated
later developments. 'If the false teacher were accustomed to
say with an imposing air, "I have seen, ah! I have seen!" in
referring to his revelations, the apostle's allusion would be
obvious and telling' (Findlay).

vainly puffed up by his fleshly mind, Paul probably
chose this phrase to drive home the fact that their asceticism
and angel worship, far from securing the destruction of the
flesh, proved that they were even controlled by the flesh in the
very faculty which stood furthest from it.

*V*19: **and not holding fast the Head, from whom all the
body, being supplied and knit together through the
joints and bands, increaseth with the increase of God.**

and not holding fast the Head, Paul here attacks the superior
claims of the false teachers by showing that their attachment
to Christ was purely nominal. 'They profess to be in "the
body" indeed, but to have found a method of growth
superior to that available for the *hoi polloi* of Christians'
(Lukyn Williams). But none are exempt from the general law
that makes the growth of all the members depend upon their
vital union with the Head, and this also implies that each

individual member sustains an immediate relation to the Head. Hence they 'who feel concern for their salvation ought never to turn their eyes from their Head: for if they are plucked away from him by the wiles of seducers, there is an end of salvation' (Davenant).

from whom the whole body supported and held together by sinews and ligaments, (Arndt-Gingrich) In *Eph* 4.16 Paul uses the same 'body' metaphor to illustrate the co-operation of the members in relation to their mutual dependence on the Head; whereas here he sets forth the absolute primacy of the Head in order to show that no member of the body can live, let alone grow, in separation from its Head. 'The difference corresponds to the different aims of the two epistles. In the Colossian letter the vital connexion with the Head is the main theme; in the Ephesian, the unity in diversity among the members' (Lightfoot).

increaseth with the increase of God. This is the increase that God bestows through Christ, in whom is 'all the fulness of the Godhead' [*v* 9]. 'Growth from God, and in conformity with Him, is only to be obtained by holding fast to Christ' (Lukyn Williams).

*V*20: **If ye died with Christ from the rudiments of the world, why, as though living in the world, do ye subject yourselves to ordinances,**

Since you died with Christ to the basic principles of this world, why, as though you still belonged to it, do you submit to its rules: (NIV) The interpretation of this verse depends upon our understanding of the key phrase, 'the rudiments (or elements) of the world'. Many commentators favour the rendering, 'the elemental spirits of the universe'

(RSV), because they maintain that such a reference to these astral deities is particularly apt in a passage which refutes angel worship. But A. J. Bandstra asks the pertinent question, 'Does Paul elsewhere say that Christians have died to the angelic, cosmic or demonic powers?' He certainly predicts the final abolition of these powers [1 Cor 15.24], and proclaims their present defeat by Christ [v 15], 'but nowhere does he speak of believers having died to them. On the other hand, the Apostle does specifically assert that Christians have died to the law [Gal 2.19; Rom 7.4].' Moreover, when Paul here asks the question, 'Why as living in the world are you *dogmatized*?' (cf v 14: 'the *dogmata* [i.e. the law of ordinances] which were against us') 'the parallels of *Rom* 8.12 and 7.6 suggest themselves, where Paul states that Christians are no longer debtors to live according to the flesh, and that they have been discharged from the law, which once held them captive, so that they no longer serve according to the old written code'. Hence Bandstra concludes that Paul chose the term 'not only because it aptly described what for him were the basic forces of the world, namely the law and the flesh, but also because these forces formed the point at which Jewish and Gentile religion met' (*The Law and the Elements of the World*, pp. 68–71).[1]

Thus Paul is exhorting the Colossians to live out the faith they confessed in their baptism: Since you then died with Christ and put off the body of flesh [vv 11, 12; cf 3.3], you must no longer behave as though you were still subject to the basic principles of this world – those religious regulations

1. Compare the usage in Gal. 4.3, 9 which is consistent with this interpretation. Herman Ridderbos also rejects the 'cosmic' view, because this verse clearly shows that Paul is thinking 'of the sin-dominated world of men, in which believers are no longer to "live" (which can scarcely be said of the cosmos as universe)' (*Paul – An Outline of His Theology*, p. 149).

[*vv* 21, 22] – which are powerless to save and are weak and defenceless before sin.

*V*21: **Handle not, nor taste, nor touch 22 (all which things are to perish with the using), after the precepts and doctrines of men?**

Paul's scornful reference to the 'No trespassing' signs set up by the false teachers shows that a negative asceticism has nothing in common with the gospel. These prohibitions are arranged in an ascending order of stringency – 'Do not take it, do not even taste it, do not so much as touch it!' (Beet) – and are condemned by the apostle on two counts. 1. To abstain from things which are destined to perish with the using cannot possibly promote superior holiness [1 *Cor* 8.8]. 'The thought is that these things which are merely material, as is shown by their dissolution in the ordinary course of nature, have in themselves no moral or spiritual effect' (Abbott). [*Matt* 15.17] 2. To submit to the arbitrary rules of men is to exchange gospel liberty for legal bondage [*Is* 29.13; *Mark* 7.7]. 'We are free from men not that we may please ourselves, but that we may please Him' (Maclaren). [1 *Cor* 7.23].

*V*23: **Which things have indeed a show of wisdom in will-worship, and humility, and severity to the body;** *but are* **not of any value against the indulgence of the flesh.**

but they are of no value, serving only to indulge the flesh. (RSV margin) The ending of this difficult verse is problematical, but the alternative rendering given here is strongly supported by F. W. Beare and W. Hendriksen, and it has the advantage of bringing the argument to a more forceful conclusion. Paul concedes that such ascetic regulations have indeed an appearance of wisdom, but in reality those who practise the precepts of men pamper 'the flesh' instead of subduing it. For the false wisdom of the 'fleshly' mind finds outward expression in 'self-imposed' worship, spurious 'humility', and unsparing treatment of the body. This unnatural denial of the needs of the body not only ignores the great gospel command, 'Do thyself no harm' [*Acts* 16.28], but also ministers to the very pride which it was designed to mortify. 'The carnal nature is all the while gratified, even though the body, wan and wasted, is reduced to the point of bare existence. There is more pride in cells and cloisters than in courts and palaces, and oftentimes as gross sensuality. The devotee deifies himself, is more to himself than the object of his homage ... The entire phenomenon, whatever its special aspect, is a huge self-deception, and a reversal of that moral order which God has established' (Eadie).

CHAPTER THREE

Since the Colossians were raised with Christ and their true life is now hid with Christ in God, they must set their minds on heavenly things, for when the exalted Christ appears they shall also appear with him in glory [vv 1–4]. Therefore they must put to death the sins that belonged to the old life, seeing that they have put off the old man with his doings, and have put on the new man who is being renewed after the image of his Creator; before whom there are no distinctions of race or class since Christ is in all alike [vv 5–11]. As God's elect they must therefore put on all the Christian graces, especially love, peace, and thankfulness. They are to let the word of Christ so dwell in them that they will be enriched in wisdom, edified in worship, and prompted to praise [vv 12–17]. Finally the mutual duties of wives and husbands, parents and children, masters and servants, are each to be regulated by their relation to the Lord [vv 18–4.1].

*V*1: **If then ye were raised together with Christ, seek the things that are above, where Christ is, seated on the right hand of God.**

As usual in Paul, 'therefore' (here rendered 'then') marks the transition to exhortation [cf *Rom* 12.1; *Eph* 4.1]. 'If' implies no uncertainty, but means 'if, as is the case' or 'since'. Having explained the significance of union with Christ in his death [2.20], Paul now shows that the same bond unites all the

[64]

members with the resurrection-life of their Head. The reference is not primarily to the subjective experience of his readers, but to the objective benefit which this eschatological event secured for them. The Colossians had entered into conscious possession of this new life by faith and baptism. And since baptism is the visible symbol of union with Christ [*Rom* 6.3ff], it becomes for believers 'the demonstrable line of demarcation between the old and the new, and faith in the gospel means a new self-judgment, that of being dead to sin and alive to God' (Ridderbos, *Paul*, p. 214).

seek the things that are above, where Christ is, In thus directing the Colossians to 'seek the things that are above', Paul again may be using a slogan of the false teachers in a 'disinfected' sense (H. Chadwick). Instead of heeding such claims to a secret knowledge of heavenly mysteries [2.18], they must realize that they have already been raised to heaven with Christ [*Eph* 2.6], and that their true life is now 'hid with Christ in God' [*v* 3]. Hence they must seek to live in a manner which befits those who belong to this supernal realm with all its transcendent realities [*Phil* 3.19f]. 'The exhortation is simply to an actual life consonant with our change of state ... It is an exhortation to us to be in life real citizens of the heavenly kingdom to which we have been transferred; to do the duties and enter into the responsibilities of our new citizenship' (B. B. Warfield, 'The Hidden Life', *Faith and Life*, pp. 352–3).

seated on the right hand of God. This clause sets forth the completeness of the Saviour's work and the dignity of his position in language which is clearly derived from *Ps* 110.1 [cf *Heb* 1.3, 13; 8.1; 10.12; 12.2; 1 *Pet* 3.22; *Rev* 3.21]. 'Session at the right hand of God means joint-rule. It thus implies divine dignity, as does the very fact of sitting in God's presence' (W. Foerster, *TDNT*, Vol. III, p. 1089).

V2: Set your mind on the things that are above, not on the things that are upon the earth.

This deepens the thought of the previous verse: 'You must not only *seek* heaven; you must also *think* heaven' (Lightfoot). Since earthly thoughts will never sustain a heavenly walk [*Phil* 3.19], Paul urges them so to set their mind upon things above that the whole of their attitude towards earthly things will be determined by this heavenly orientation [*Matt* 6.21]. 'The apostle does not urge any transcendental contempt of things below, but simply asks that the heart be not set upon them in the same way, and to the same extent, in which it is set upon things above. The pilgrim is not to despise the comforts which he may meet with by the way, but he is not to tarry among them, or leave them with regret. "Things on earth" are only subordinate and instrumental – "things above" are supreme and final' (Eadie). This antithesis thus condemns the asceticism of the false teachers whose boastful claims to higher knowledge were nullified by their grovelling attachment to 'the basic principles of the world' [2.20f].

V3: For ye died, and your life is hid with Christ in God.

For when you renounced the old life in baptism, you then died to all its claims over you, and now that you have put on the new man 'your life is hid with Christ in God'. Here the primary idea is not that of security, but of the present concealment of our essential life. 'The world knows neither Christ nor Christians, and Christians do not even fully know themselves' (Bengel). But though the new life is hidden from the world, and in part from the believer himself, his union with

Christ means that he partakes of all the fulness of God [2.9]. If the anatomist cannot even lay bare the principle of physical life, then how much more elusive is the believer's spiritual life both as to its *origin* and *destiny*? 'As to the former, it is hidden with Christ in God; and as to the latter, it shall not be fully revealed till Christ come the second time in glory. But it shall be ultimately disclosed' (Eadie).

V4: **When Christ, *who is* our life, shall be manifested, then shall ye also with him be manifested in glory.**

The abrupt use of 'when' without a connective brings out the hope more vividly, and fills the reader 'with a sudden light' (Bengel). As Lightfoot points out, this verse is an advance on the preceding statement ('your life is hid with Christ') in two respects: 1. It is not enough to have said that the life is shared *with* Christ. The Apostle declares that the life *is* Christ [cf 1 John 5.12]; 2. '*Our*' replaces 'your' as Paul 'hastens to include himself among the recipients of the bounty'.

The Colossians are thus assured that when Christ appears, then they too will appear with him 'in glory'. Although Paul does not stop to define the content of the term, the dominant thought in this context would appear to be the investment of believers with the resurrection body of glory [cf *Rom* 8.17; *Phil* 3.20f; 1 *John* 3.2]. 'At present the real dignity of the sons of God is hidden from the eyes of men and indeed from their own eyes, as Christ is hidden from mortal sight. In that day Christ in His essential grandeur will appear and with Him will appear also the grandeur with which He will adorn His servants' (Beet).

V5: **Put to death therefore your members which are upon the earth: fornication, uncleanness, passion, evil desire, and covetousness, which is idolatry;**

In coming to the practical application, it is possible that Paul echoes an early catechism, in order to remind the Colossians of the teaching which was delivered to them before their baptism [*vv* 5–14]. As they had died to the old life of sin when they identified themselves with Christ's death in baptism, so they must put to death the earthly 'members' which are here virtually identified 'with the sins of which they were formerly the instruments' (Bruce). [cf *Rom* 6.19; 7.23] Thus the indicative, 'Ye died' [*v* 3], underlies the imperative, 'Put to death', and 'the assurance of the indicative is the urge and the incentive to the fulfilment of the imperative' (John Murray, *Principles of Conduct*, p. 220).

To the sexual sins that were so characteristic of the Graeco-Roman world – immorality, impurity, erotic passion, and evil desire – Paul adds the unrecognized sin of covetousness which he equates with idolatry because the grasping self-seeker makes material gain his god [1 *Tim* 6.10]. 'Impurity and covetousness may be said to divide between them nearly the whole domain of human selfishness and vice' (Lightfoot).

*V*6: for which things' sake cometh the wrath of God upon the sons of disobedience:

In keeping with his teaching in Rom.1.18ff. Paul declares that these sins call forth the righteous wrath of God who cannot regard this assault upon his holiness with calm indifference. This verse affords no comfort to those modern scholars who wish to personalize 'wrath' in the interests of excusing God from what they deem to be an unworthy emotion. Paul expressly affirms that this is 'the wrath *of God*', and thus points to the most intense, personal response to sin within the divine being [cf *John* 3.36; *Eph* 5.6; *Rev* 19.15]. But whereas the passage in Romans speaks of the present manifestation of God's wrath, the reference here is probably to its final outpouring on 'the day of wrath' [cf *Rom* 2.5]. Although the phrase 'upon the sons of disobedience' is strongly attested, many textual critics regard it as an interpolation from *Eph* 5.6, but it is required to complete the sense and should be retained (so Beet, Abbott, Lenski, and R. E. O. White).

*V*7: **wherein ye also once walked, when ye lived in these things;**

Or rather: **amongst whom ye also once walked,** (ASV margin) Paul's readers once walked with the sons of disobedience and travelled along the same broad way when they used to live in these vile sins. 'They then went along a path trodden by those whose character is derived from, and determined by, the principle of rebellion against God. This justifies the exhortation of verse 5, and prepares a way for that of verse 8' (Beet). [cf *Eph* 2.3]

*V*8: **but now do ye also put them all away: anger, wrath, malice, railing, shameful speaking out of your mouth: 9 lie not one to another;**

'But now' that grace has wrought such a marvellous change in the Colossians, they must discard all the sins of the old life, just as they would cast away a filthy garment. It is difficult to distinguish between 'anger' and 'wrath', though Lightfoot says the former 'denotes a more or less settled feeling of hatred' and the latter 'a tumultuous outburst of passion'. 'Malice' is the malignity that seeks to harm one's neighbour. This ill-will is publicly proclaimed in destructive speech [*Matt* 12.34]. 'Railing' is the slander by which another's character is defamed. 'Shameful speaking' is the abusive speech which is itself an abuse of the precious gift of language, and is therefore a form of utterance 'quite unfit for *a Christian mouth*' (Findlay). [cf 4.6] Paul follows his warning against these vices with a particular injunction against lying. Believers are no longer to lie to one another, because as the parallel passage shows, they are 'members one of another' [*Eph* 4.25]. As their fellowship is founded upon the truth, lies are bound to injure the body to which they belong, and so they must renounce the corrupt and corrupting deceit which was characteristic of the old man.

*V*9b: **seeing that ye have put off the old man with his doings, 10 and have put on the new man, that is being renewed unto knowledge after the image of him that created him:**

Paul reminds the Colossians of the significance of the faith confessed in their baptism, for by identifying themselves with the eschatological events of Christ's death and resurrection they had put off the old man and put on the new man. These terms are used by the apostle to express the corporate categories of his thought. The old man is what we once were in Adam, and the new man is what we have become in Christ. The headship of Adam guaranteed solidarity in sin and condemnation, but the coming of Christ introduced a new humanity created after the image of its redeeming Head [1.15]. It is only because believers have put off the old man and his doings that they can be urged to put on those Christian graces which belong to the new man [*vv* 12ff]. Thus the order of grace is not 'Do and live' but 'Live and do'.

that is being renewed unto knowledge But even though believers have already put on the new man, they are not yet perfect and are still under the necessity of being progressively renewed unto that full knowledge of God, which they are destined to attain 'in Christ' [cf *Eph* 4.13]. Unlike the speculative knowledge of the false teachers, a true knowledge of God is always intensely practical, since it includes 'the knowledge of His will in all the relations of life' (Lukyn Williams). [cf 1.9]

after the image of him that created him: The new man, like the first Adam, is created in God's image [*Gen* 1.27]. But as that image is now made known to us only in the second Adam, he becomes the pattern of the new man [1.15; *Rom* 8.29; 2 *Cor* 3.18]. 'Renewal after the image of God comes about therefore through the fact that the believer in baptism [*Gal* 3.27] puts on Christ and thus the new man . . . For this reason to be created after the image of God is the equivalent of bearing, reflecting, being transformed after the image of Christ' (Ridderbos, *Paul*, p. 225).

*V*11: **where there cannot be Greek and Jew, circumcision and uncircumcision, barbarian, Scythian, bondman, freeman; but Christ is all, and in all.**

In this new humanity the old distinctions that still divide mankind have ceased to count, for differences of race and religion (like Greek and Jew), or of culture (like Greek and barbarian), or of social standing (like slave and free) present no barrier to union with Christ. Such distinctions neither prevent the putting on of the new man, nor do they modify the possession of spiritual privilege and blessing, and this is the glory of Christianity! 'The graces of civilization are not the necessary soil for the graces of the Spirit. Secular enfranchisement is not indispensable to fellow-citizenship with the saints. In the sphere of the new man, those distinctions which obtain in the world exercise no disturbing or preventive influence' (Eadie). The enumeration here suggests that Paul has the special circumstances of his readers very much in mind [cf *Gal* 3.28]. The inclusion of the Greeks and the uncircumcised counters the Jewish element in the Colossian heresy, as 'barbarian' serves to dismiss its stress on superior knowledge, while the case of Onesimus would make the reference to slave and freeman especially relevant [4.9; *Phil* 10].

Greek and Jew, circumcision and uncircumcision, The racial antipathy which existed between Greek (Gentile) and Jew was largely due to their religious differences [*Eph* 2.11ff], but the opening of the door of faith to the Gentiles involved the abolition of these inherited privileges and the rite which represented them [*Acts* 10.28; 1 *Cor* 7.19; *Gal* 5.6, 6.15]. 'If it is no advantage to be born a Jew, it is none to become as a Jew' (Lightfoot).

barbarian, Scythian, This is not an antithesis, but a climax. The Scythians, 'more barbarous than the barbarians' (Bengel), were 'little better than wild beasts' (Josephus). 'Barbarian' reflects the contempt of the Greek for the language of the 'uncultured', for he regarded their unintelligible utterances as mere sounds without sense ('bar-bar!'). The eminent linguist Max Müller, who traced the beginning of the science of language from the first Day of Pentecost, wrote: 'Not till that word *barbarian* was struck out of the dictionary of mankind and replaced by *brother*, not till the right of all nations of the world to be classed as members of one genus or kind was recognized, can we look even for the beginnings of our science. This change was effected by Christianity.'

bondman, freeman; Although the *status quo* of slaves is maintained by Paul both in this letter [*v* 22–4.1] and that to Philemon, his insistence upon their equal standing in Christ dealt a fatal blow to the idea that a slave was no more than 'a human tool' (Aristotle).

but Christ is all, and in all. 'Christ' stands at the 'end of the sentence, with accumulated emphasis. The Church regards and values each man in his relation to Christ, and bids every other consideration bow to this. He is "all things" – our common centre, our standard of reference, and fount of honour, the sum of all we acknowledge and desire; and he is "in all" – the common life and soul of his people, the substance of all we experience and possess as Christians' (Findlay).

*V*12: **Put on therefore, as God's elect, holy and beloved, a heart of compassion, kindness, lowliness, meekness, longsuffering;**

Paul follows the demand to renounce the habits of the old life with the positive command to put on the virtues that characterize the new man. The phrase, 'as God's elect', brings the fact of their eternal election to bear upon their present behaviour. It is evident that God's sovereign choice obliges us to put on all the virtues which he recommends to us in the following words. 'For this very thing is the aim and end of his Election, as the Apostle elsewhere informs us, when he saith, That *GOD hath elected us in CHRIST, that we might be holy and blameless before him, Eph* 1.4' (Daillé). Moreover, as 'holy and beloved' indicates, their election consecrated them to God's service and gave the proof of God's love. These three titles – elect, holy, beloved – are taken from the Old Testament and transferred 'from the Israel after the flesh to the Israel after the Spirit' (Lightfoot). Since the church is a mixed community, the virtues listed by Paul all have to do with personal relationships, and are designed to promote peace and harmony amongst those who by background and temperament were once poles apart.

a heart of compassion, In this, as in everything else, Christ is our supreme example [*Matt* 9.36; *Mark* 1.41; *Luke* 7.13]. It took Christian compassion to transform the brutal and brutalizing world in which lack of feeling was the Stoic ideal. A heart of compassion is found 'in every regenerate person: he is therefore moved at the very first view of another's misery' (Davenant).

kindness, lowliness, These are linked because the Christian's attitude towards others is partly determined by his own view of himself (*Phil* 2.3). 'Kindness', says R. C. Trench, is a beautiful grace 'pervading and penetrating the whole nature, mellowing there all which would have been harsh and austere.' Although Augustine was unmoved by the preaching of Ambrose, he confessed that he was won by the Bishop's kindness: 'And I began to love him, not at first as a teacher of the truth, which I despaired of finding in Thy Church, but as a fellow-creature who was kind to me.' The pagan mind admired self-assertion and despised humility, but Christianity elevated it into a virtue. 'A noble sense was put into the word by the spirit of Christ. Pride has vanished. Others are not beneath our feet. We ourselves are poor sinners. We do not lower ourselves while we are great, as Chrysostom thought; we know that we are *not* great, hence we never even pretend that we are great. So we move among men' (Lenski).

meekness, longsuffering; These denote the exercise of the Christian temper in its outward bearing towards others. They are best distinguished by their opposites. The first is opposed to 'rudeness, harshness'; the second to 'resentment, revenge, wrath' (so Lightfoot). L. H. Marshall notes that 'meekness' has two elements in it: 1. a consideration for others [see *Gal* 6.1; 1 *Cor* 11.33; 12.14, 15; *Phil* 2.4]; 2. a willingness to waive an undoubted right [1 *Cor* 9.18]. The real meaning of 'long-suffering' is better conveyed by 'long-temperedness'. It refers 'to the endurance of wrong and exasperating conduct on the part of others without flying into a rage or passionately desiring vengeance. One of the great ethical qualities of God celebrated in Holy Scripture is that He is "slow to anger", and Paul here suggests that the spiritual man shares in this characteristic of God' (Marshall, *The Challenge of New Testament Ethics*, p. 294).

*V*13: **forbearing one another, and forgiving each other, if any man have a complaint against any; even as the Lord forgave you, so also do ye:**

Paul next enforces the need for mutual forbearance and forgiveness in the Christian community: 'forbearing *one another* and forgiving *yourselves*'. As Vincent remarks, 'The latter pronoun emphasizes the fact that they are *all* members of Christ's body – everyone members one of another – so that, in forgiving *each other* they forgive *themselves*.' This forgiveness is to be as full and free as the divine forgiveness, for in 2.13 Paul uses the same word which literally means 'to grant grace'. The second part of the verse shows that Christ's forgiveness to us is 'the model, and therefore the motive, of our forgiveness of others' (Beet).

*V*14: **and above all these things** *put on* **love, which is the bond of perfectness.**

Above all these, the Colossians are to don the pre-eminent grace of love, which is 'the bond producing perfection'

(Moulton-Turner). Others regard love as the bond which binds all the other virtues together, but as the context underlines the unity of the community, it is preferable to see love as the cohesive grace which binds believers together. *'Love, then, is "the bond of perfection" in the sense that it is that which unites believers, causing them to move forward toward the goal of perfection'* (Hendriksen). [*Eph* 4.13]

*V*15: **And let the peace of Christ rule in your hearts, to the which also ye were called in one body; and be ye thankful.**

The word represented by 'rule' means literally 'to act as umpire', and from Paul's use of the same word in 2.18 it would seem that he had in mind the umpire who awarded the prize to the winner in athletic contests. The false teachers wished to set themselves up as umpires by awarding the prize for obedience according to their own false standards, but Paul says that the true umpire is within the hearts of believers. This is that peace with God which Christ made through the blood of his cross [1.20]. Instead of heeding the spurious demands of these charlatans, the Colossians must listen to the one authentic umpire, Christ's own peace ruling in their hearts.

to the which also ye were called in one body; Since the goal of their calling is the harmony of the body to which they belong, each member must so acknowledge the headship of Christ [1.18] that no alien spirit is allowed to disturb his reign of peace [cf *Eph* 4.3, 4]. 'Strife is the inevitable result when men are out of touch with Him who is the one Source of true peace; but there is no reason why those who have accepted the peace which Christ established by His death on the cross should have any other than peaceful relations among themselves' (Bruce).

and be ye thankful. As the best preservative of this peace, Paul urges them to be always thankful that God has delivered them from the power of darkness and transferred them into the church, which is the domain of Christ's kingly rule [1.13]. 'The command *to give thanks* prevails in this Epistle, as that *to rejoice* in Philippians' (Findlay). [1.3; 2.7; 3.15, 17; 4.2]

*V*16: **Let the word of Christ dwell in you richly; in all wisdom teaching and admonishing one another with psalms *and* hymns *and* spiritual songs, singing with grace in your hearts unto God.**

Let the word of Christ dwell in you richly as you teach and counsel one another with all wisdom, (NIV) In comparing this with the closely linked passage in *Eph* 5.18, 19, we find that the command to be filled with the Spirit is here replaced by 'Let the word of Christ dwell in you richly'. 'In view of the parallelism involved we are bound to conclude that the filling of the Spirit and the richly indwelling Word of Christ are functionally equivalent. That indwelling Word is not some specialized or restricted truth granted only to some in the congregation but "everything I have commanded you" [*Matt* 28.20], faithfully believed and obeyed ... The reality of the Spirit's filling work is the reality, in all its breadth and richness, of the ongoing working of Christ, the life-giving Spirit, with his Word. To look for some word other than this Word, now inscripturated for the church, is to be seeking some spirit other than the Holy Spirit' (Richard B. Gaffin, *Perspectives on Pentecost*, pp. 33–4). Thus the fellowship of believers is founded upon their mutual submission to 'the word of Christ', the reception of which is marked by the response of praise (as the NIV makes clear). This verse does not therefore mean that believers receive instruction solely by means of song!

and as you sing psalms, hymns and spiritual songs with gratitude in your hearts to God. The importance of singing in the worship of the early church is illustrated in a letter written by Pliny to the Emperor Trajan about AD 112. He reports that the Christians of his province gathered regularly on a fixed day before dawn to sing antiphonally 'a hymn to Christ as God'. It is doubtful whether the terms here used by Paul can be clearly distinguished. 'Psalms' may point to the Christian adoption of the Old Testament Psalter, but in 1 *Cor* 14.26 an ecstatically inspired hymn is evidently in view. 'Hymns' were probably like the samples of Christian praise that seem to be embedded in the New Testament [e.g. *Eph* 5.14; 1 *Tim* 3.16]. 'Spiritual songs' are so designated to show the source of their inspiration. However, if, as some scholars think, 'spiritual' covers all three terms, then the richness of the early church's worship is expressly attributed to the prompting of the Holy Spirit. Paul insists that such praise should ascend to God from grateful hearts because true worship always demands the response of man's whole being.

*V*17: **And whatsoever ye do, in word or in deed,** *do* **all in the name of the Lord Jesus, giving thanks to God the Father through him.**

The whole field of human conduct is covered by the injunction to 'do all in the name of the Lord Jesus'. There may well be an allusion to the commitment to live under the authority of Christ which was made in baptism [cf 1 *Cor* 6.11], for the new convert in that act of allegiance placed 'the totality of his life under Christ's lordship' (R. P. Martin). This brief command affords a more comprehensive guide to Christian living than any that could be provided by the heaviest tome of moral casuistry. In every doubtful situation the believer may find sure guidance by asking himself: 'What is the Christian thing to do here? Can I do this without compromising my Christian confession? Can I do it (that is to say) "in the name of the Lord Jesus"?' (F. F. Bruce). The place of thanksgiving in the Christian life is again stressed by Paul when he says that our actions are to be accompanied by the sacrifice of grateful praise which is to be offered through Christ, the only Mediator, in all our approaches to God.

*V*18: **Wives, be in subjection to your husbands, as is fitting in the Lord.**

Although Paul's brief 'household code' did not threaten the existing social order by offering any incitement to revolutionary change, it brought a new motivation to the old standards of conduct which leavened the lump of paganism and transformed all social relationships. By showing that the 'stronger' and 'weaker' parties in every relationship are equally accountable to Christ, Paul here lays bare their mutual obligations towards one another, for in a one-sided world it would come as a great surprise to some Christians to learn that wives, children, and slaves had rights as well as husbands, parents, and masters. In this verse wives are bidden to be in subjection to their husbands, 'as is fitting in the Lord'. Some scholars think that the reference to what is fitting points to the adoption of a Stoic maxim, but if so it is Christianized by the addition of the all-important words 'in the Lord'. According to Abbott, the apostle's use of the imperfect tense does not imply 'that the duty has not hitherto been rightly performed, but only that the obligation existed previously'. When even pagans could recognize that wives should be subject to their husbands, it would not be fitting if Christians were more reluctant to acknowledge it! Paul advances the reason for such wifely subjection in *Eph* 5.23. It is found in the headship that makes man the ruling partner in the marriage relation, an arrangement not only established by creation but also endorsed in redemption. Hence Christian wives must understand that equality within the sphere of grace [*Gal* 3.28; 1 *Pet* 3.7] does not set aside the God-given order for marriage. Nevertheless, the phrase 'in the Lord' clearly sets a limit to this obedience. For wives are only subject to their husbands in what pertains to their legitimate authority *as husbands*: 'everything not contrary to God' (Fausset).

*V*19: **Husbands, love your wives, and be not bitter against them.**

Turning now to husbands, Paul tells them to love their wives with the self-giving love (*agapaō*) that cares for all their needs [cf *Eph* 5.25ff]. 'He saith not, Rule over them, subdue them if they will not submit, but love them, and so win them to your will; make their yoke as easy as may be, for they stand on even ground with you, as yoke-fellows, though they draw on the left side' (John Trapp).

and be not bitter against them. The preposition 'against' probably suggests that what is in view is the bitterness 'vented on the wife though not caused by her' (W. Michaelis, *TDNT*, Vol. VI, p. 125). It is a mistake to regard the exhortation as an anti-climax, for many who are polite to all outsiders, 'nevertheless treat their wives and children at home with covert bitterness, because they do not fear them' (Bengel). And, as Lenski observes, this negative is also a litotes which points to the contrary virtue: 'ever be considerate toward them in the way described in *Eph* 5.28, etc.'.

*V*20: **Children, obey your parents in all things, for this is well-pleasing in the Lord.**

In addressing children Paul makes their natural obligation to obey their parents a summons to religious service: 'for this is well-pleasing in the Lord' [cf *Eph* 6.1–3]. 'The love of the child's heart naturally leads it to obedience. Only an unnatural child can be a domestic rebel. Where the parents are Christians, and govern their children in a Christian spirit, obedience should be without exception' (Eadie).

*V*21: **Fathers, provoke not your children, that they be not discouraged.**

On the other hand, fathers (upon whom the responsibility for the family primarily rests) also have a duty towards their children. [*Eph* 6.4]. They must avoid all that would irritate or exasperate the children – injustice, severity, constant fault-finding, etc. – lest they become discouraged. 'Paul is not commonly regarded as an expert in child psychology, but, where Jesus ben Sira cannot see beyond the menace of the spoilt child, Paul is sensitive to the child's need for encouragement' (G. B. Caird).

*V*22: **Servants, obey in all things them that are your masters according to the flesh; not with eye-service, as men-pleasers, but in singleness of heart, fearing the Lord:**

In bidding slaves to render uniform obedience to those who are their masters 'according to the flesh', Paul implies that there is another Master who is above the temporal limitations of the existing social order [4.1]. Although many modern versions rightly translate 'slaves', it is perhaps preferable to retain 'servants' because the exhortation 'embodies principles applicable to all posts of subordination' (E. K. Simpson). If Paul had preached 'the social gospel' he doubtless would have encouraged slaves to repudiate their position, with disastrous consequences, yet in sending the converted slave Onesimus back to his master as 'a brother beloved' [*Phil* 16] he set forth the great principle of religious equality before God which undermined and eventually brought about the abolition of slavery. So here the apostle asks for that heart-obedience which only the redeemed man is able to render to his master. As the adoption of this ethic led to a transformation of the slave/master relationship, so its widespread absence from the modern industrial scene is diagnosed by John Murray as 'our basic economic ill' (*Principles of Conduct*, p. 103).

not with eye-service, as men-pleasers, 'The vice was venial in slaves; it is inexcusable, because it darkens into theft, in paid servants – and it spreads far and wide. All scamped work, all productions of man's hand or brain which are got up to look better than they are, all fussy parade of diligence when under inspection and slackness afterwards – and all their like which infect and infest every trade and profession, are transfixed by the sharp point of this precept' (Maclaren).

but in singleness of heart, fearing the Lord. The sincere service which lacks any ulterior motives is prompted by a reverential fear of the Lord. 'Where the all-seeing Master is forgotten, we seek as our highest good the favour of men: and our service sinks down to the external forms which alone lie open to the eye of man. Thus fear of the Supreme Lord saves even the slave from degrading bondage to man' (Beet). [1 *Cor* 7.23]

*V*23: **whatsoever ye do, work heartily, as unto the Lord, and not unto men;**

'Here is the secret for all who work for other men, whether they are slaves or free employees: "Throw your soul into the work as if your one employer were the Lord!" ' (Lenski). No labour is servile when the Lord's approval is the paramount consideration. Hence the most willing service to men is rendered by those who are bent on pleasing Christ!

*V*24: **knowing that from the Lord ye shall receive the recompense of the inheritance: ye serve the Lord Christ.**

Paul is not above encouraging such hearty obedience by the prospect of an eternal reward which he describes as 'the inheritance', a significant word since slaves could not inherit any earthly possession. Faithful service is sure to be rewarded, yet this is the reward of grace and not a merited award!

Serve ye the Lord Christ. It is better to take the verb as an imperative. Paul here sums up his charge to slaves in one urgent phrase. 'Since the Lord gives such a reward so rich and blessed, serve ye Him. Look above and beyond human service, and with such a bright prospect in view, serve the Lord Christ. Your masters on earth have no absolute right over you: the shekels they may have paid for you can only give them power over your bodies, your time and your labour, but the Lord has bought you with His blood, and has therefore an indefeasible claim to your homage and service' (Eadie).

*V*25: **For he that doeth wrong shall receive again for the wrong that he hath done: and there is no respect of persons.**

As masters are reminded in *Eph* 6.9 that 'there is no respect of persons', no acceptance of a man's face, no partiality shown because of his social standing; so here slaves are warned that their low position will not protect them from the same just judgment of their misdeeds. For with the case of Onesimus in mind, Paul would not wish others to think that in pleading for the offender he condoned the offence. 'The low often think that they should be spared on account of their lowness. That is denied' (Bengel).

Ch4, v1: **Masters, render unto your servants that which is just and equal; knowing that ye also have a Master in heaven.**

Finally, Paul calls upon masters to provide their slaves with what is just and fair, because they are also accountable to the same Master in heaven. So since slaves and masters both owe obedience to the one Lord, they need stand in no doubt of how they should behave toward one another. 'The lordship of Christ dominates the whole Epistle. The assertion that the proud master who deemed his fellow-man his chattel is himself a mere *slave* of Christ, sets Christ's authority in a vivid and striking light. This consideration makes the Christian master apprehensive as to his treatment of his dependants. *He* is "in heaven", the seat of Divine authority and glory, whence he shall soon return to judgment' (Findlay).

CHAPTER FOUR

In drawing to a close, the apostle urges his readers to continue in prayer with thanksgiving, and requests them to remember his work in their prayers [vv 2–4]. A concern to present a credible witness must lead them to behave wisely and speak graciously to outsiders [vv 5, 6]. Paul warmly commends the bearers of the Epistle, Tychicus and Onesimus, and conveys the greetings of his companions [vv 7–14], He gives directions for an exchange of letters between Laodicea and Colossae, and instructs Archippus to fulfil his ministry [vv 15–17]. As usual Paul adds the final greeting in his own hand, and movingly asks them to remember his bonds [v 18].

V2: Continue steadfastly in prayer, watching therein with thanksgiving;

As prayer is the first mark of the Christian life [*Acts* 9.11], so perseverance in prayer is the essential element for continued growth in grace [*Eph* 6.18]. In calling the Colossians to unceasing prayer, Paul directs them to be watchful in it. It is better to regard this as an independent command. The meaning is not, 'Watch and be attentive during prayer!' but: 'Pray, and at the same time be watchful!' (so Lenski). [*Matt* 26.41]. Such constant watchfulness is necessary to avoid being overtaken by any sudden temptation. 'With thanksgiving' again brings in the characteristic refrain of this Epistle [cf 1.2; 2.7; 3.15, 17]. Gratitude for Christ's great salvation must be expressed in heart-felt praise! 'Ceaseless prayer combined with ceaseless praise was the atmosphere of Paul's spiritual life' (Beet).

*V*3 : **withal praying for us also, that God may open unto us a door for the word, to speak the mystery of Christ, for which I am also in bonds; 4 that I may make it manifest, as I ought to speak.**

Paul also requests prayer for himself and his helpers that God may open unto them a door of opportunity for effective evangelism [1 *Cor* 16.9; 2 *Cor* 2.12]. 'God opens the door by his providence. Many fail to note this and try to open doors for themselves. When we are spreading the gospel we must follow God's providential indications as to where we ought to work' (Lenski). [cf *Acts* 16.7, 9].

to speak the mystery of Christ, for which I am also in bonds; It was because Paul had proclaimed 'the mystery of Christ' to the Gentiles that he was now a prisoner in chains (see comment on 1.26, 27 and compare *Eph* 3.1ff). Paul 'might have been still at large, if he had been content to preach a Judaic Gospel. It was because he contended for Gentile liberty, and thus offended Jewish prejudices, that he found himself a prisoner' (Lightfoot). [*Acts* 21.28; 22.21, 22; 24.5, 6; 25.6, 8].

that I may make it manifest, as I ought to speak. Since the revelation is made in proclamation, Paul desires to be endued with the requisite grace to do justice to the gospel [1.25ff]. Significantly he makes no request for deliverance from suffering, for he regards what he endures for the sake of the church as a part of his vocation [1.24]. 'If Paul felt his conception of the greatness of the gospel dwarfing into nothing *his* words when he tried to preach it, what must every other true minister of Christ feel?' (Maclaren).

V5: **Walk in wisdom toward them that are without, redeeming the time.**

In regard to those who are outside the church, Paul counsels believers to 'walk in wisdom', 'neither giving offence carelessly, nor taking offence causelessly' (Trapp). They must remember that they are constantly under the critical scrutiny of these 'outsiders' and be conscious of their great responsibility towards them [cf I *Cor* 10.32]. All too often Christians deservedly earn the reputation of being a 'peculiar' people! 'We owe them that are without such a walk as may tend to bring them in. Our life is to a large extent their Bible. They know a great deal more about Christianity, as they see it in us, than as it is revealed in Christ, or recorded in Scripture – and if, as seen in us, it does not strike them as very attractive, small wonder if they still prefer to remain where they are' (Maclaren).

buying up the opportunity. (ASV margin) This means an 'intensive buying', i.e. 'a buying which exhausts the possibilities available' (F. Büchsel, *TDNT*, Vol. I, p. 128). As Christians have a duty to their unbelieving neighbours, they must seize every opportunity for witnessing to the faith, and use it to the full [cf *Eph* 5.16].

V6: **Let your speech be always with grace, seasoned with salt, that ye may know how ye ought to answer each one.**

Let your speech always be gracious, seasoned with salt, (Hendriksen) Christians are not only to commend the gospel by their lives but also by their lips [*Ps* 45.3; *Luke* 4.22]. They must always be distinguished by the winsomeness of their speech, which is to be further enhanced by being 'seasoned with salt'. 'Profane men have their saltiness, but he is not speaking of them ... for he reckons as tasteless everything that does not edify' (John Calvin). Paul probably has in view both the use of salt as a preservative from corruption [*Eph* 4.29; 5.4], and its function in making food more palatable [*Luke* 14.34].

that ye may know how ye ought to answer each one. 'Not only must your conversation be opportune as regards the time; it must also be appropriate as regards the person' (Lightfoot). No effective witness is given to Christ by rattling off a stereotyped testimony, because this completely ignores the fact that each person has his own special needs. It is worth noting that Paul constantly adapted his speech to his audience [*1 Cor* 9.22].

*V*7: **All my affairs shall Tychicus make known unto you, the beloved brother and faithful minister and fellow-servant in the Lord: 8 whom I have sent unto you for this very purpose, that ye may know our state, and that he may comfort your hearts; 9 together with Onesimus, the faithful and beloved brother, who is one of you. They shall make known unto you all things that *are done* here.**

The bearer of this letter to the Colossians and of all the news from Rome is Tychicus [*Acts* 20.4], Paul's beloved brother and a trusted helper and fellow-servant 'in the Lord', whose ministry is certain to encourage and strengthen their hearts. In our idiom 'I have sent' means 'I am sending' [cf NIV]. Maclaren draws attention to the indispensable service Tychicus performed in delivering this letter. 'Small things done for Christ are great ... What is the use of writing letters, if you cannot get them delivered? It takes both Paul and Tychicus to get the letter into the hands of the people at Colossae.'

With Tychicus Paul is returning the runaway slave Onesimus, whose misdeeds are here blotted out by the gracious designation, 'the faithful and beloved brother'. Onesimus could not be placed on a par with Tychicus for the faithfulness of his service, but only for the faithfulness of his belief in the Lord who saved him from his former slavery to sin. As this faith makes him a member of the redeemed community ('who is one of you'), Paul is confident that he will be welcomed by the Colossian church and pardoned by his wronged master Philemon.

*V*10: **Aristarchus my fellow-prisoner saluteth you, and Mark, the cousin of Barnabas (touching whom ye received commandments; if he come unto you, receive him), 11 and Jesus that is called Justus, who are of the circumcision: these only *are my* fellow-workers unto the kingdom of God, men that have been a comfort unto me.**

Paul next sends the greetings of six persons who are with him as he writes [*vv* 10–14]. The fact that Paul here names Aristarchus [*Acts* 19.29; 20.4; 27.2] as his 'fellow-prisoner' but transfers the title to Epaphras in *Phil* 23 may mean that these men took turns in voluntarily sharing the apostle's imprisonment in order to minister to his needs. Paul's commendation of Mark [cf 2 *Tim* 4.11] is apparently in connection with a projected visit to the churches of Asia, but we are left in the dark as to whether this mission was initiated by Paul or someone else. Although Mark's desertion from the first missionary journey led to a sharp contention between Paul and Barnabas

[*Acts* 15.36–41], he had evidently regained Paul's respect by his subsequent service and vindicated his kinsman's confidence in him. It is a strange irony that an otherwise unknown believer, 'Jesus who is called Justus', should have achieved the kind of posthumous fame that many strive for in vain simply because he wanted to send his greetings to the Christians at Colossae!

These three Jewish Christians have proved a comfort to Paul, for they are the only Jews in Rome who are really working with him for 'the kingdom of God' (in contrast to the profitless exertions of the Judaizers!). This pathetic complaint, which confirms what Paul hints at elsewhere [cf *Phil* 1.15–17], shows that the rest of the Jews there were hostile to his gospel, though many of them hailed Jesus as their Messiah. 'Even when he was a prisoner, their unrelenting antagonism pursued the Apostle. They preached Christ of "envy and strife". Not one of them lifted a finger to help him, or spoke a word to cheer him. With none of them to say, God bless him! he toiled on. Only these three were large-hearted enough to take their stand by his side, and by this greeting to clasp the hands of their Gentile brethren in Colossae and thereby to endorse the teaching of this letter as to the abrogation of Jewish rites' (Maclaren).

*V*12: **Epaphras, who is one of you, a servant of Christ Jesus, saluteth you, always striving for you in his prayers, that ye may stand perfect and fully assured in all the will of God.**

Since Aristarchus, Mark, and Jesus named Justus are the only Jews Paul mentions, Epaphras, Luke and Demas must be Gentiles [*vv* 12–14]. As a native of Colossae and as the founder of the church there [1.7], Epaphras is well described as 'one of you'. In conveying the greeting of this slave of Christ Jesus,

Paul informs them that he is always wrestling in prayer on their behalf [v 2]. 'The effort of Epaphras' prayers was like the intense effort of a Greek athlete contending for a prize. The appropriateness of this phrase is felt by all to whom prayer is a reality' (Beet).

that ye may stand perfect and fully assured in all the will of God. The content of Epaphras' prayers virtually sums up the teaching of the letter. As against the false quest for perfection by legalistic supplements [2.20f], he asks that they may stand firm in the faith [1.23; cf *Eph* 6.11, 13], finding their maturity in the all-sufficient Christ [2.9, 10]. And instead of seeking to complete their faith by some higher revelation, he prays that they may be fully assured 'in all the will of God' [cf 2.2].

*V*13 : **For I bear him witness, that he hath much labour for you, and for them in Laodicea, and for them in Hierapolis.**

Paul's insistence upon the faithfulness of Epaphras' labours for the Colossian Christians and those in the neighbouring cities of Laodicea and Hierapolis (see Introduction), may be intended to forestall any possible criticism of his having gone to Rome to misrepresent the situation in Colossae or to escape from his responsibilities there. 'This is an example of a good pastor, whom distance cannot induce to forget the Church or prevent him from carrying the care of it with him beyond the sea' (Calvin).

*V*14 : **Luke, the beloved physician, and Demas salute you.**

Luke was one of Paul's closest friends. He was an almost constant companion of the apostle from the time of the second

[91]

missionary journey (as is shown by the 'we' sections in *Acts* 16.10–17; 20.5–21.18; 27.1–28.16) until the end of his life [*2 Tim* 4.11]. Over the years there were doubtless numerous occasions when Paul had reason to be grateful for Luke's professional skill as a doctor, and perhaps not least during his imprisonment in Rome. The fact that both the writers of the Second and Third Gospels were with Paul at this time clearly 'disproves the contention of those who say that Paul knew next to nothing about the historical Jesus' (A. M. Hunter).

Here Demas salutes the Colossians, but in the last crisis he forsook Paul and returned to Thessalonica 'having loved this present world' [*2 Tim* 4.10]. 'We are not better than the Apostles. If all the light of their wisdom and miracles, could not keep *Demas* from becoming bankrupt of the truth, we ought not to think it strange, if there happen to be among us, some whom belly and vanity do precipitate into the like fault, notwithstanding the clearness and evidence of our holy doctrine' (Daillé).

V15: **Salute the brethren that are in Laodicea, and Nymphas, and the church that is in their house.**

Paul now asks the Colossians to pass on his greetings to the believers in Laodicea, 'and to Nympha and the church in her house' (NIV). Lenski thinks that this house-church was in Hierapolis, because it would be so unlike Paul not to extend a greeting to the Christians there [*v* 13]. Be that as it may, Nympha must have been a wealthy woman to have a house large enough to allow the young church to gather for worship in it. No buildings were set apart for public worship until the third century, and so the early Christians were obliged to hold their services in private houses [cf *Rom* 16.5; *1 Cor* 16.9; *Acts* 12.12].

*V*16: **And when this epistle hath been read among you, cause that it be read also in the church of the Laodiceans; and that ye also read the epistle from Laodicea.**

The letter 'from Laodicea' is probably the one we know as 'Ephesians', for its impersonal nature suggests that it was intended as a circular letter. It is clear from *Eph* 6.21, 22 that Tychicus was also the bearer of this letter, and since he had to pass through Laodicea on his way to Colossae, he would leave a copy there before delivering the Colossian letter. This verse not only shows that Paul's letters were intended to be read to the assembled company of believers when they met for worship [1 *Thess* 5.27], but also that they were from the first intended for a wider circulation than their initial destination would imply.

*V*17: **And say to Archippus, Take heed to the ministry which thou hast received in the Lord, that thou fulfil it.**

It seems that Archippus was a member of Philemon's family, possibly his son. In *Phil* 2 Paul gives him the honourable title of 'fellow-soldier', and it is reasonable to assume that the church appointed him to be their pastor when Epaphras left for Rome. In thus publicly endorsing the appointment and encouraging him to fulfil his ministry, Paul probably had in mind the urgent need to defend the truth of the gospel by dealing decisively with the errors propagated by the false teachers (so R. P. Martin).

*V*18: **The salutation of me Paul with mine own hand. Remember my bonds. Grace be with you.**

To mark the letter as genuine Paul now adds the final greeting in his own handwriting [2 *Thess* 3.17]. 'Remember my bonds' is not an appeal for sympathy, but an exhortation to obey the teaching of this letter. 'His bonds establish an additional claim to hearing. He who is suffering for Christ has a right to speak on behalf of Christ' (Lightfoot). [cf *Eph* 3.1; 4.1; 6.20; *Phil* 9, 13] Paul's last word to the Colossians is his prayer that *the* grace of the one authentic gospel which he preaches, may be with them. This very brief benediction is found only here and in 1 *Tim* 6.21, 2 *Tim* 4.22.

INTRODUCTION TO PHILEMON

Lightfoot maintains that this Epistle holds a unique place in Paul's writings because 'it is the only strictly private letter which has been preserved'. But the greetings at the beginning and end of the letter suggest that it was intended for a public hearing. Hence this brief epistle is to be seen not simply as a private letter from one personal friend to another, but rather 'as an apostolic letter about a personal matter' (R. P. Martin). For though the letter is the very model of tact and courtesy, it is also the authoritative utterance of Christ's apostle, and Paul makes it clear to Philemon that he expects him to do even more than he asks [v 21].

Paul writes to Philemon to intercede for his runaway slave Onesimus [v 10]. Apparently he robbed his master and headed straight for Rome, but instead of finding refuge in the crowded city, he somehow came into contact with Paul and was converted. The once worthless slave now began to live up to his name, and proved so 'profitable' [v 11] to Paul that he would have liked to keep him as his friend and helper, if he had not felt obliged to return him to his wronged master in Colossae. But because the slave who ran away as a pagan is returning as a Christian, Philemon is asked to grant far more than a mere pardon to the repentant Onesimus, for he is to receive him as 'a brother beloved' [v 16]. It can be safely assumed that Philemon did respond to Paul's appeal, since he would not have kept a letter which he refused to obey.

Onesimus was converted at about the same time that Paul received news from Epaphras of the threat to the faith which had arisen in Colossae. Paul therefore entrusted Tychicus with the responsible task of protecting Onesimus from arrest by slave catchers on the return journey [*Col* 4.9], and of delivering the letters to the Laodiceans (probably our 'Ephesians', see comment on *Col* 4.16) and the Colossians, together with this covering letter to Philemon.

Although it is often remarked that Paul stops short of asking Philemon to give Onesimus his freedom, it may be questioned whether the thought ever crossed Paul's mind, for in the social conditions of the time emancipation could be a doubtful boon amounting only to the freedom to starve. But if this letter presented no revolutionary challenge to the social structures of the day, the implications of its teaching were bound to prove fatal to slavery in the end.

The outstanding value of this short Epistle is helpfully summarized by W. Graham Scroggie under seven heads. 'Its Personal value consists in the light which it throws upon the character of Paul. Its Ethical value consists in its balanced sensitiveness to what is right. Its Providential value consists in its underlying suggestion that God is behind and above all events. Its Practical value consists in its application of the highest principles to the commonest affairs. Its Evangelical value consists in the encouragement it supplies to seek and to save the lowest. Its Social value consists in its presentation of the relation of Christianity to slavery and all unchristian institutions. And its Spiritual value consists in the analogy between it and the Gospel Story' (*Know Your Bible*, Vol. II, p. 201).

PHILEMON

Paul links Timothy with himself in greeting Philemon, his family and the church in his house [vv 1–3]. He thanks God for the news of Philemon's faith in Christ and love for the saints which has given him much joy [vv 4–7]. As Christ's prisoner, Paul appeals to Philemon on behalf of Onesimus, who has become his own son in the faith. The once unprofitable slave is now so profitable that Paul would have preferred to keep him, if he had not been under the obligation of returning him to his master [vv 8–14]. Paul suggests that the desertion of Onesimus was overruled so that Philemon might receive back a brother beloved instead of a slave [vv 15, 16]. He pleads with Philemon to refresh his heart by receiving Onesimus, and offers to repay any debts incurred by the fugitive slave, though he reminds Philemon of his even greater debt to himself [vv 17–20]. He is confident that Philemon will do more than he asks, and expresses the hope that he will soon be a guest at Philemon's home [vv 21, 22]. As usual Paul conveys the greetings of his companions, and concludes the letter with the benediction [vv 23–25].

V1: **Paul, a prisoner of Christ Jesus, and Timothy our brother, to Philemon our beloved and fellow-worker, 2 and to Apphia our sister, and to Archippus our fellow-soldier, and to the church in thy house:**

By introducing himself as 'a prisoner of Christ Jesus' [vv 9, 10, 13, 23], Paul enlists the sympathy of Philemon and implicitly contrasts his own suffering with the trifling sacrifice he is asking him to make. 'How could Philemon resist an appeal which was penned within prison walls and by a manacled hand?' (Lightfoot). Since Paul had never been to Colossae, Philemon was presumably converted during Paul's ministry in Ephesus [v 19], where he must have also met Timothy [*Acts* 19.22]. The greetings sent by Timothy thus serve to remind Philemon that fellow-believers are bound together in the bonds of brotherhood. But it is clear that Timothy played no part in the composition of the letter because Paul speaks in the singular from verse 4. Moreover, there is special significance in addressing Philemon as 'our beloved', for it is a reminder that he belongs to a community of mutual love [v 9; *Rom* 1.7], which is patterned upon the self-giving love of the One who gave himself for its salvation [*Eph* 5.25]. Hence Philemon must extend that same love to the slave whom Paul calls 'a brother beloved' [v 16]. Philemon is also Paul's 'fellow-worker', and as such he shares in the common task of witnessing to the gospel by word and deed [vv 5, 7], and by consecrating his house to Christ's service [v 2].

Apphia, a 'sister' in the Lord, is evidently Philemon's wife. As the lady of the house she had to supervise the duties of the slaves, and so her own response to Paul's appeal for Onesimus would be a crucial factor in influencing the decision of her husband. In a letter addressed to a Christian 'household', it is fair to assume that Archippus is Philemon's son. If *Col* 4.17 means that he was given pastoral responsibility in the absence of Epaphras, this would explain why the younger man is described by the stronger term – 'fellow-soldier' – which 'seems to indicate an activity requiring more pains and self-denial' (Theodor Zahn). J. Knox's idea that Archippus was the master of Onesimus and the real recipient of the letter is an exegetical flight of fancy which is unworthy of the serious attention it has received. The return of Onesimus would also concern the 'church' [*Col* 4.15] which gathered in Philemon's house, 'because it was in that congregation that Onesimus would have to be recognized as a Christian. Further, some at least of the worshippers there would be his fellow-servants, with whom he must be properly reinstated' (Lukyn Williams).

V3: **Grace to you and peace from God our Father and the Lord Jesus Christ.**

Paul greets all the believers at Philemon's house and prays that they may enjoy grace and peace 'from God our Father and the Lord Jesus Christ' – a formula that shows the *source* of these blessings. Grace is the unmerited favour of God which brings sinners to salvation in Christ, and peace is that state of spiritual well-being that flows from the reception of this grace. 'There is no grace unless God bestows it, and there is no real peace unless it flows forth from God's reconciliation with sinful man' (J. J. Müller).

V4: **I thank my God always, making mention of thee in my prayers,**

Paul's thanksgivings fulfil a function similar to that of the overture in an opera, for they introduce the themes to be elaborated in the body of the letter (J. Knox). So in *vv* 4–7 no fewer than seven of the terms used by Paul are later taken up and woven into his argument: 'love' [*vv* 5, 7, 9, 16]; 'prayers' [*v* 22]; 'sharing', 'partner' [*v* 17]; 'the good', 'goodness' [*v* 14]; 'heart' [*vv* 12, 20]; 'refreshed' [*v* 20].

I thank my God always, Since God alone is the author of salvation, Paul does not congratulate Philemon on having conducted himself as a Christian, but gives God all the praise which is his due. Moreover, Paul not only thanks God for what he has already accomplished in Philemon's life, he also prays that God will complete the good work which he has begun in his heart [*Phil* 1.6].

V5: **hearing of thy love, and of the faith which thou hast toward the Lord Jesus, and toward all the saints;**

Presumably Paul heard of Philemon's faith and love from Epaphras [*Col* 1.7, 8; 4.12]. 'Love is first mentioned, as more noticed. But faith is the mother-grace, the womb wherein love and all the rest of that heavenly offspring are conceived' (Trapp). Paul is glad that Philemon is so forward in showing love for all the saints because he is about to ask for a further demonstration of it [*vv* 9, 16]. This emphasis upon love results in a criss-cross arrangement of the clauses in the sentence (*chiasmus*):

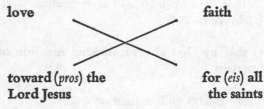

| **love** | **faith** |
| **toward** (*pros*) **the Lord Jesus** | **for** (*eis*) **all the saints** |

V6: **that the fellowship of thy faith may become effectual, in the knowledge of every good thing which is in you, unto Christ.**

(praying) **that the sharing to which your faith gives rise may effectively impart the knowledge of every good things that is in us and that leads us closer to Christ.** The meaning of almost every word in this difficult verse is disputed. But if 'fellowship' is here taken as 'sharing', then Paul is praying that the generosity which was prompted by Philemon's faith might promote 'the knowledge of every good thing which is in us'. This is not some form of theoretical enlightenment; it is that concrete knowledge of 'the good' which God desires believers to perform [*Rom* 12.2; *Gal* 6.10; 1 *Thess* 5.15]. Paul is thus preparing Philemon for the request that follows, so that his 'goodness should not be as of necessity, but of free will' [*v* 14]. And by acting out what God's grace has first worked in, Philemon will be drawn closer to Christ. Alternatively, 'unto Christ' may mean that this deed will advance Christ's cause and so serve to glorify him.

V7: For I had much joy and comfort in thy love, because the hearts of the saints have been refreshed through thee, brother.

Paul speaks of the great joy and comfort he had in the news of Philemon's love. This love appears to have found active expression in a particular deed by which 'the hearts of the saints have been refreshed'. No doubt Philemon had used his wealth to minister to the needs of his fellow-believers in some time of crisis, and this may have been in connection with the great earthquake of AD 60. By placing 'brother' last in the sentence, Paul turns this one word into a highly effective appeal. As Philemon had shown himself to be a true Christian brother in the past, he is again called to live up to this description by the way in which he received Onesimus.

V8: Wherefore, though I have all boldness in Christ to enjoin thee that which is befitting, 9 yet for love's sake I rather beseech, being such a one as Paul the aged, and now a prisoner also of Christ Jesus:

Since Paul has been given impressive proof of Philemon's love, he will not invoke his authority as an apostle to command what ought to be done. He prefers to entreat 'for love's sake'. This phrase does not refer to the love of Philemon or Paul, but to 'love absolutely, love regarded as a principle which demands a deferential respect' (Lightfoot). Paul reinforces his appeal by reminding Philemon that it is made by an old man who is also a prisoner for the sake of Christ. 'Such is the man who now forbears to use his indisputable authority and merely makes a request' (Beet). Although some versions prefer 'ambassador' (RSV, NEB), it is virtually certain that Paul means 'old man', since he would not use an official title in making what is essentially a personal appeal. There is no ground for doubting the accuracy of the description, for at this time Paul would be nearly sixty, and prematurely aged by his sufferings.

V10: I beseech thee for my child, whom I have begotten in my bonds, Onesimus,

After having so carefully prepared the way, Paul at last comes to the purpose of the letter. He again uses the verb 'I beseech', but this time mentions the object of his request. He is appealing to Philemon on behalf of his child, whom he has begotten in his bonds [1 Cor 4.15]. Paul's use of this expression does not mean that 'it was done by his own power, but only through his instrumentality; for it is not the work of any man to reshape and renew a human soul in the image of God, and it is with this act of spiritual regeneration that he is now dealing' (Calvin).

This tactful preamble is designed to enlist Philemon's sympathy before Paul dramatically reveals the name of his child: 'It is Onesimus!' (Moffatt). Paul's plea for Onesimus is often compared with the letter written by Pliny the Younger in which he asks Sabinianus to forgive his freedman for having run away. But though both letters deal with a similar situation, the contrasts are more striking than the resemblances. Pliny is uncertain of the future good conduct of the freedman, but Paul has no doubt about the slave's. In assuming that Sabinianus will be justly angry, Pliny begs him not to resort to torture; whereas Paul not only counts on Philemon's forgiveness but also expects him to receive his slave as a brother beloved [v 16]. Pliny sternly threatened the freedman, but there is no hint that Paul spoke severely to the slave (so Scroggie). Pliny's letter appeals to Stoic virtue, but Paul's reckons on the response of Christian love.

V11: who once was unprofitable to thee, but now is profitable to thee and to me:

Onesimus, whose name means 'profitable', must have rendered very grudging service to his master before his flight. But Paul here assures Philemon with a playful touch of humour that the slave who had once been *unprofitable* to him is now *profitable* to them both [*Col* 3.22ff; v 13]. 'Christianity knows nothing of hopeless cases. It professes its ability to take the most crooked stick and bring it straight, to flash a new power into the blackest carbon, which will turn it into a diamond' (Maclaren).

V12: whom I have sent back to thee in his own person, that is, my very heart:

This verse shows the strength of Paul's affection for his new son in the faith [v 10]. 'In Onesimus, Paul sends his own heart, a part of himself, all his own tender emotions as they are centred in Onesimus. Can there be a question as to how Philemon will treat what Paul sends him?' (Lenski).

V13: whom I would fain have kept with me, that in thy behalf he might minister unto me in the bonds of the

gospel: 14 but without thy mind I would do nothing; that thy goodness should not be as of necessity, but of free will.

Onesimus gave evidence of the great change in his life by serving Paul so faithfully that he would have liked to keep him. And though the imprisoned apostle might well have claimed such service from Philemon in the person of his slave, he resolved to do nothing without Philemon's consent so that his goodness would not appear constrained but freely willed. It is because love cannot be compelled that Paul refuses to intrude on a decision that must be Philemon's own (so Lohse). Some have thought that Paul is here asking Philemon for the return of Onesimus. But in the light of what follows [*vv* 15, 16], his deliberately vague reference to 'thy goodness' evidently means that 'Philemon's kindly reception of Onesimus must not even *seem* to be constrained' (Vincent).

*V*15: **For perhaps he was therefore parted *from thee* for a season, that thou shouldest have him for ever;**

Instead of fixing Philemon's attention upon the desertion of Onesimus, Paul uses a euphemistic expression which suggests that God had overruled this evil for good. 'He does not say *he parted himself*, but *he was parted*: since the design was not Onesimus' own to depart for this or that reason: just as Joseph also, when excusing his brethren, says [*Gen* 45.5] *God did send me hither*' (Chrysostom as cited by Lightfoot). Hence it seems that God's purpose in this brief parting was that Philemon might enter into a new relationship with Onesimus which not even death could dissolve [*v* 16].

*V*16: **no longer as a servant, but more than a servant, a brother beloved, specially to me, but how much rather to thee, both in the flesh and in the Lord.**

Although Onesimus was still a slave, he could no longer be treated merely as a slave, for he was far more than that. The relationship between master and slave is now on an entirely different plane, because both are in Christ [1 *Cor* 7.21–24; *Col* 3.11]. The grace of God has made the slave 'a brother beloved'. Onesimus is especially loved by Paul, but how much more should this be true of Philemon, since Onesimus belonged to him in the double sense of being both his slave and his brother. 'In the flesh Philemon had the brother for a slave; in the Lord he had the slave for a brother' (H. A. W. Meyer).

*V*17: **If then thou countest me a partner, receive him as myself.**

If then Philemon considers Paul as his 'partner' [*v* 6], a sharer in the same faith, he is to receive Onesimus as he would the apostle himself! For to do otherwise would be to deny the reality of that bond which makes all believers fellow-members of the body of Christ.

*V*18: **But if he hath wronged thee at all, or oweth *thee* aught, put that to mine account;**

What Paul only expresses hypothetically is in fact the case, for Onesimus must have robbed Philemon of a considerable sum to have paid for the long journey to Rome. To remove this obstacle to their reconciliation, Paul himself undertakes the responsibility for the debt and asks Philemon to charge it to his account. But though the offer is made in all seriousness, the next verse shows that Paul did not really expect it to be taken up.

*V*19: **I Paul write it with mine own hand, I will repay it: that I say not unto thee that thou owest to me even thine own self besides.**

Here Paul takes up the pen from his amanuensis, and presents Philemon with his signed IOU. This promise to pay would be legally binding, but the creditor is at once reminded that he owes much more than a sum of money, even *his own self*! Philemon's obligation to Paul thus far exceeds the loss he had sustained through Onesimus, for he owed his salvation to Paul's ministry. And as this is a claim which can never be repaid, Paul is confident that Philemon will not press him for the payment of the lesser debt. 'By putting it this way, Paul wishes to remind Philemon of the pardon he himself received, to make him understand how grace freely received calls to remission of debt, when a fellow sinner also comes to conversion' (C. Bouma cited by Müller).

*V*20: **Yea, brother, let me have joy of thee in the Lord: refresh my heart in Christ.**

The confirmatory particle 'yea' gathers up all that Paul has said on behalf of Onesimus, and introduces a final personal plea to Philemon: 'let me have some benefit from you in the Lord' (Arndt-Gingrich). He who owes the right to be called 'brother' to Paul's ministry is now able to bring some benefit to his benefactor by receiving back the slave as his 'brother' in the same family of faith [*v* 16]. Since Philemon had refreshed the hearts of the saints with his deeds of love [*v* 7], he must not neglect this opportunity of refreshing Paul's heart. The phrases 'in the Lord' and 'in Christ' are perhaps meant to remind Philemon that only the Lord could enable him to show such grace to the one who had wronged him.

[106]

*V*21: **Having confidence in thine obedience I write unto thee, knowing that thou wilt do even beyond what I say.**

Paul is writing with every confidence in Philemon's obedience, but as the apostle has chosen to entreat rather than command [*v* 8], the obedience in view here must be that of the disciple to his Lord. With the earthly master's obedience to his Master in heaven thus assured, Paul knows that Philemon will do even more than he says. To understand this as a veiled request to give Onesimus his freedom is certainly rash. As it is enough for Paul to have shown that Onesimus is a brother to be loved, he refuses to specify how that love is to be expressed, and this is left entirely to the Christian judgment of his friend.

*V*22: **But withal prepare me also a lodging: for I hope that through your prayers I shall be granted unto you.**

Since Paul evidently anticipates an early release from prison, he asks Philemon to prepare a guest room for him. 'There is a gentle compulsion in this mention of a personal visit to Colossae. The Apostle would thus be able to see for himself that Philemon had not disappointed his expectations' (Lightfoot). Paul expresses the hope that God will answer the prayers of the church ('your' is plural) on his behalf, so that he may be soon restored to them. According to *Phil* 2.24, Paul was planning to visit Macedonia after being set free, and perhaps he intended to come to Colossae via Macedonia. Although he makes no mention of travelling west to Spain [*Rom* 15.23, 24], the testimony of Clement (AD 95) suggests that he fulfilled this long cherished ambition before he was again arrested and brought back to Rome to suffer death at the hands of Nero (*c* AD 67).

*V*23: **Epaphras, my fellow-prisoner in Christ Jesus, saluteth thee; 24 *and so do* Mark, Aristarchus, Demas, Luke, my fellow-workers.**

Five of Paul's companions send their greetings (see comments on *Col* 4,10–14), but here he calls Mark, Aristarchus, Demas, and Luke his fellow-workers. Calvin says of the later desertion of Demas: 'And if one of Paul's assistants became weary and discouraged and was afterwards drawn away by the vanity of the world, let none of us rely too much on our own zeal lasting even one year, but remembering how much of the journey still lies ahead, let us ask God for steadfastness.'

*V*25: **The grace of our Lord Jesus Christ be with your spirit. Amen.**

After addressing Philemon in the singular from verse 4, Paul reverts to the plural 'your' as he prays that Christ's grace may rest on the entire community who will hear the letter read out as they meet for worship [*v* 2]. Paul's loveliest letter is thus brought to a fitting conclusion with the same word of 'grace' which is his mint-mark in every Epistle.

Soli Deo Gloria

BIBLIOGRAPHY

Abbott, T. K., *The Epistle to the Ephesians and to the Colossians* (ICC)
  (T & T Clark, 1897)
Arndt, W. F., and Gingrich, F. W., *A Greek–English Lexicon of the
  New Testament* (University of Chicago Press, 1957)
Bandstra, Andrew James, *The Law and the Elements of the World*
  J. H. Kok, Kampen, 1964)
Beare, Francis W., *The Epistle to the Colossians* (IB) (Abingdon, 1955)
Beet, J. Agar, *A Commentary on St. Paul's Epistles to the Ephesians,
  Philippians, Colossians, and to Philemon* (Hodder & Stoughton,
  1890)
Bengel, J. A., *New Testament Word Studies* (Kregel, 1971)
Bruce, F. F., *Commentary on Romans* (Tyndale, 1963)
Caird, G. B., *Paul's Letters from Prison* (New Clarendon Bible)
  (OUP, 1976)
Calvin, John, *Galatians – Colossians* (St. Andrew Press, 1965)
  (Translator, T. H. L. Parker)
Calvin, John, *Second Corinthians – Philemon* (St Andrew Press, 1964)
  (Translator, T. A. Smail)
Clowney, Edmund P., *The Doctrine of the Church* (Presbyterian &
  Reformed, 1969)
Daillé, Jean, *Sermons on Colossians* (London, 1672)
Davenant, John, *An Exposition of the Epistle of Paul to the
  Colossians* (Hamilton Adams, 1831/2)
Douglas, J. D. (Editor), *The New Bible Dictionary* (IVP, 1962)
Eadie, John, *Commentary on the Epistle of Paul to the Colossians*
  (Zondervan, 1957)

BIBLIOGRAPHY

Fausset, A. R., *Ephesians* (JFB) (Collins, 1874)

Fergusson, James, *A Brief Exposition of the Epistles of Paul* (The Banner of Truth Trust, 1978)

Findlay, G. G., *Colossians* (Pulpit Commentary) (Kegan Paul, Trench, 1886)

Gaffin, Richard B., *The Centrality of the Resurrection* (Baker Book House, 1978)

Gaffin, Richard B., *Perspectives on Pentecost* (Presbyterian & Reformed, 1979)

Guthrie, Donald, *New Testament Introduction* (Tyndale, 1970)

Guthrie, Donald, *Colossians* (NBC) (IVP, 1970)

Hendriksen, William, *Colossians and Philemon* (NTC) (The Banner of Truth Trust, 1971)

Henry, Matthew, *Commentary on the Holy Bible* (various editions)

Hunter, A. M., *Galatians – Colossians* (LBC) (SCM Press, 1966)

Kittel, G. and Friedrich, G., *Theological Dictionary of the New Testament* Vols. I–X (Eerdmans, 1964–76) (Translated by Geoffrey W. Bromiley; index by Ronald E. Pitkin)

Knox, John, *The Epistle to Philemon* (IB) (Abingdon, 1955)

Lenski, R. C. H., *The Interpretation of Colossians and Philemon* (Augsburg, 1964)

Lightfoot, J. B., *St. Paul's Epistles to the Colossians and to Philemon* (Zondervan, 1961)

Lohse, Eduard, *Colossians and Philemon* (Hermeneia) (Fortress Press, 1971)

Maclaren, Alexander, *The Epistles of Paul to the Colossians and Philemon* (Hodder & Stoughton, 1888)

Marshall, L. H., *The Challenge of New Testament Ethics* (Macmillan, 1946)

Martin, Ralph P., *Colossians: The Church's Lord and the Christian's Liberty* (Paternoster Press, 1972)

Martin, Ralph P., *Colossians and Philemon* (NCB) (Oliphants, 1974)

Moule, C. F. D., *The Epistles to the Colossians and Philemon* (CGT) (CUP, 1957)

Moule, H. C. G., *Colossians and Philemon* (CUP, 1893)

Müller, J. J., *The Epistles of Paul to the Philippians and to Philemon* (NICNT) (Eerdmans, 1955)

Murray, John, *Collected Writings* Vol. 2 (The Banner of Truth Trust, 1977)

Murray, John, *Principles of Conduct* (Tyndale, 1957)

Pink, Arthur W., *Gleanings from Paul* (Moody Press, 1967)

Poole, Matthew, *Commentary on the Holy Bible* Vol. 3 (The Banner of Truth Trust, 1963)

Radford, Lewis B., *The Epistle to the Colossians and the Epistle to Philemon* (WC) (Methuen, 1931)

Ridderbos, Herman, *Paul – An Outline of his Theology* (Translation by John Richard De Witt) (Eerdmans, 1975)

Robbins, Ray F., *Philemon* (BBC) (Broadman Press, 1971)

Robinson, J. Armitage, *St. Paul's Epistle to the Ephesians* (James Clarke, n.d.)

Rupprecht, Arthur A., *Philemon* (EBC) (Zondervan, 1978)

Scroggie, W. Graham, *Know Your Bible* Vol. II (Pickering & Inglis, 1956)

Simpson, E. K., and Bruce, F. F., *Ephesians and Colossians* (NICNT) (Eerdmans, 1957)

Trapp, John, *Commentary on the New Testament* (Sovereign Grace Book Club, 1958)

Trench, R. C., *Synonyms of the New Testament* (James Clarke, 1961)

Vaughan, Curtis, *Colossians* (EBC) (Zondervan, 1978)

Vincent, Marvin R., *The Epistles to the Philippians and Philemon* (ICC) (T & T Clark, 1972)

Vincent, Marvin R., *Word Studies in the New Testament* (MacDonald, n.d.)

Warfield, B. B., *Faith and Life* (The Banner of Truth Trust, 1974)

White, R. E. O., *Colossians* (BBC) (Broadman Press, 1971)

Williams, A. Lukyn, *The Epistles of Paul the Apostle to the Colossians and Philemon* (CGT) (CUP, 1907)

Wilson, R. McL., *Gnosis and the New Testament* (Basil Blackwell, 1968)

Yamauchi, Edwin, *Pre-Christian Gnosticism* (Tyndale, 1973)

Zahn, Theodor, *Introduction to the New Testament* Vol.I (Klock & Klock, 1977).